W9-BXS-635

PRACTICING THE BIBLICAL FEASTS

Celebrating the Biblical Feasts within the Christian Church Calendar at Home

Dawn S. Gilmore

ISBN 978-1-63885-410-4 (Paperback)
ISBN 978-1-63885-411-1 (Digital)

Covenant Books, Inc.
11661 Hwy 707
Murrells Inlet, SC 29576
www.covenantbooks.com

Lovingly dedicated to my gracious and most loving husband, Glenn, who has put up with all my decorations, let me "play house," and eaten every one of the recipes with delight!

CONTENTS

Foreword...7

Preface..9

Acknowledgments 15

Introduction...17

Chapter 1:   Why Is Any of This Important? 21

Chapter 2:   The Year Begins: Rosh Hashanah, Yom Kippur........37

Chapter 3:   Sukkot: The Feast of Tabernacles............47

Chapter 4:   Advent, Hanukkah and the Christmas Season.........53

Chapter 5:   Epiphany and Ordinary Time (Part 1) 73

Chapter 6:   Ash Wednesday, Lent, Purim 76

Chapter 7:   Holy Week, Passover, Feast of
             Unleavened Bread, Easter......................88

Chapter 8:   Shavuot, Pentecost, Ordinary Time (Part 2).............99

Appendix 1: The Recipes...113

Appendix 2: Liturgies for the Feasts..........................180

       Rosh Hashanah/Yom Kippur 180

       Sukkot 186

       A Brief Liturgy for Advent at Home....................187

       Hanukkah..192

       The Story of Purim—The Feast of Lots (Long Version) 200

       Purim—Feast of Lots (Short Game Version) 214

       Passover Haggadah.......................................217

       Shavuot/Pentecost..243

Bibliography...247

There is a movement within the Christian church today that has encouraged contemporary worshipers to be interested and open to engaging in ancient forms of worship. We have seen musicians introducing revamped and retuned versions of older hymns. We have seen prayers and practices from the ancient church reintroduced in modern worship. The regular observance of the Lord's Supper, use of lectionary scripture readings, and the incorporation of candles have found their way into *nonliturgical* worship gatherings. There are even signs that the observance of the Christian year as a way of keeping time is slowly making its way back into the worship of Protestant-free church traditions. Although the Christian year has its origins in the ancient church, many are finding that it is still as applicable today as it was in previous centuries.

The Christian year calendar is the foundation for most of Christian worship as well as a central component to Christianity as it focuses on the retelling of the Christ events: the anticipation of his coming, his birth, life, death, resurrection, ascension, and future reign. The centrality of time in Christian worship instructs us on how we should organize our lives around following Christ and telling others about Jesus and informs us as to the way in which we should worship. As a result, the Christian year is not simply a way for the Christ follower to mark time, but it is a spiritually forming aspect of our worship. In corporate worship, we come together to remember the fullness of God's story allowing his story to affect the way we live and worship.

This book is a welcome resource for the church. The connections made between the Jewish feasts and the Christian year calendar reveal for us God's story and grand plan for this creation. Throughout the book, we are reminded of our past, challenged in the present, and encouraged toward deeper growth in Christ for the future. The practical elements of recipes and worship liturgies for the specific feasts are a welcome addition and make this a unique resource. As you read this book and utilize its materials, enjoy learning and worshiping with others as you feast upon the Lord.

Steven D. Brooks
Director, Worship Quest Ministries
Author, *Worship Formation: A Call to Embrace Christian Growth in Each Element of the Worship Service*

PREFACE

I *love* holidays! Holidays mean lots of things! It means a day off for most people. It's a chance to do something different. Opportunities to sleep late, get together with friends, forget about work for a short time, and celebrate whatever! Our government has made it so that most of our civic holidays fall on a Friday or Monday so that we can have a long weekend. Some holidays are really date specific, like the fourth of July, and can land on any day of the week. We have other celebrations in life that may have deep significance for us, personally, but are not considered holidays (most unfortunate, I think!). Birthdays and anniversaries fall into this category.

So what does "holiday" mean? Originally, the word came from "holy day" which meant a day set aside for a special religious observance.[1]

According to the dictionary, the first known usage of the word was before the twelfth century.[2] In Scripture, we find the words *sacred times*, *festivals*, *feasts*, and *Sabbath*. All are words that describe a time that is set aside for a particular thing to be celebrated or commemorated.

In our American culture, we take our holidays seriously! We celebrate with vigor! The marketing of our holidays has also had a huge impact on our lives as we are bombarded with advertisements of sales, great deals on goods and services, as well as how we should be celebrating. We celebrate with food and entertainment.

---

[1]   www.merriam-webster.com/dictionary/holy%20day
[2]   Logos Bible Software. *The Lexham Bible Dictionary*, Feasts and Festivals of Israel.

Our national holidays include the following:

- New Year's Day
- Martin Luther King Day
- President's Day
- Memorial Day
- Independence Day
- Labor Day
- Thanksgiving Day
- Christmas Day

These are days most people get a day off from work. We have other celebrations that are not "official" holidays but are days of celebration as well.

- Valentine's Day (February 14)
- St. Patrick's Day (March 18)
- Flag Day (June 14)
- Halloween (October 31)
- D-Day (December 7)
- New Year's Eve (December 31)

There are also the religious holidays that most churches observe. These may or may not also be national holidays. Depending on the denomination, some of the church feasts may or may not be observed. Some churches also include national holidays into their liturgy. It is fascinating how our workweek and holidays came to be.

In 1908, a New England mill became the first American factory to institute the five-day week. It did so to accommodate Jewish workers, whose observance of a Saturday Sabbath forced them to make up their work on Sundays, offending some in the Christian majority. The mill granted these Jewish workers a two-day weekend, and other factories followed this example. The Great Depression cemented the two-day weekend into the economy, as shorter hours were considered a remedy to underemployment.[3]

The study of our holiday history is most interesting. The study of the church's cycle of seasons is also most interesting as these help us in our spiritual journey of faith as a fellowship of Christ followers within a community throughout the year. I challenge you to consider how including the biblical feasts might also be rewarding, uplifting, and encouraging in your spiritual journey as you begin to learn about them and put them into practice within the context of your family and friends.

I love my heritage, and my mother, especially, was instrumental in my knowing and understanding about my heritage. I am part Dutch, English, Belgian, French, and Jewish. My maternal grandfather came to America from Austria. My maternal great-grandparents came from the Netherlands. My paternal great-grandparents and great-great-grandparents came from various parts of Europe. Throughout my childhood, many of the holidays associated with my heritage were celebrated. It has become part of my normal routine in any given year to include at least a few of the celebrations with my family. I grew up with the mantra, "Treat your family like company and your company like family." So designing celebrations and entertaining large groups of friends, family, and students have become a no-brainer for me!

I became more interested in my Jewish heritage while in college. I was asked to lead a devotional in a small group that I was part of in my dorm. I went to the library and began to do some research on the meaning of Hanukkah, specifically on the meaning of lighting the candles. That was the beginning of my developing a richer understanding of that particular celebration.

---

[3]   Phil Sopher, "Where the 5-Day Workweek Came From." August 21, 2014. (www.theatlantic.com/business/archive/2014/08/where-the-five-day-workweek-came-from/378870/ accessed 6/25/2019).

Our wedding was a mix of culture! We were married under a *chuppah* (a canopy) in a Nazarene church, and my father, a Baptist minister, officiated. We had all the bases covered!

In the early years of our marriage, I introduced our circle of friends to the celebrations of Passover and Hanukkah. In fact, when we lived in Seattle, we had a close circle of friends that celebrated all our various heritages by having dinner parties with ethnic foods that represented our various ethnicities. We felt like we traveled the world through food! We learned so much about each other's cultures through these monthly dinner parties.

My husband and I have moved many times during the course of our marriage for work-related reasons. A great benefit to having lived in so many places is that we developed lifelong friendships. Wherever we lived, we welcomed people to share in our celebrations that were specific as well as nonspecific. My husband's passion has always been people and ministry. My passion has been in teaching music but also in biblical studies. (I began reading through the Bible at an early age. By the time I was eleven, I had read Catherine F. Vos's *The Child's Story Bible* from cover to cover twelve times!) I taught music in Christian schools and, in many of those years, would take time to teach my choir students about some of the biblical festivals as they related to Christian holy days. At Christmastime, I would talk about Hanukkah, the miracle of the lights, and the story of persecution and a band of brothers that led an uprising for the freedom to worship the One true God in the place that he had designated. At Easter time, I would give a demonstration of a *Seder* (Passover meal) complete with all the food elements and invite brave students to taste the *maror*—the horseradish sauce! I would tell them the story of redemption using the elements on the *Seder* plate to describe how God had led his people out of Egypt, gave them commandments to live by, and taught them to worship him alone. I would show them how all of these elements also represent what God had done through Christ, his Son, by giving his life in exchange for ours. In our repertoire of music, we sang songs that reflected the themes from scripture.

When I began teaching at the Bible college, I enjoyed teaching about the practices of the Christian year. As I taught about the cycle of the Christian year, I also incorporated the biblical feasts. I invited students to our home to celebrate the feasts of Hanukkah and Passover.

I had always been interested in learning more about the church year, and as I had also always been involved in the music ministry of the church, I would pay attention to the various seasons and use that to guide my worship planning. Down deep in my being, I desired to learn more about the seasons and cycles of the church year. In 2011, I embarked on a longtime dream to begin a doctoral program in worship studies. I found myself between jobs, so it seemed that the time was finally right to do this! The Robert E. Webber Institute for Worship Studies was exactly the program and course of study I wanted! Through my studies, I learned even more about the seasons of the church year and why they are important for us today. It's not just a liturgical or "high church" thing. It's about living spiritually in the seasons of life, during the course of a year, and how that has an impact on how we live every day. It's also not just a Sunday thing or a denomination thing. If you are serious about your faith journey as a follower of Christ, then you should want to develop a life of spiritual practices that help you know God and deepen your understanding and relationship with him.

Putting all of these things together, the seasons of the church year and the biblical feasts, into my life has been an amazing journey. Life is full of ups and downs; it certainly is never boring! Participating in God's story through the seasons and festivals is enriching to my spiritual life and, I hope, the life of my family and friends who participate with me.

As I finish writing this book, COVID-19 has overtaken our world. It has had a huge impact on worship at church. It has also had an impact on family celebrations. As you read through these chapters, keep in mind that everything has been scaled back this year of 2020! So most of the descriptions of recent celebrations are from earlier years. That being said, as I finish writing at the end of 2020, it occurs to me that worship at home is even more important to foster. The church may be forever changed going forward. All I know for certain is that it is *my* responsibility to choose to follow the Lord's direction and to worship and give glory to him in all I do.

Do you desire to know more of God? Are you willing to try, perhaps, some new practices that will aid your spiritual development and enrich your relationship with Jesus the Messiah? Do you desire these things for your family? For your church family? If so, read on!

ACKNOWLEDGMENTS

I want to acknowledge with gratitude my aunt Martha Amster Hodges who has been my partner in crime for most all our lives! We have tried and tested the recipes, filled our homes with special decorations and food, invited family and friends to join in as we have celebrated our Jewish heritage together!

I also want to thank the rest of my family, my students, as well as friends who have joined us through the years at our table for many of these feasts and celebrations. You were honored guests as we desired to engage in a deeper understanding of God's story.

This past year, for our adopted son's birthday, we decided to give him a DNA kit. When we adopted him at the age of eleven, we were given few details about his heritage. We have always celebrated our heritages and cultures, and Paul has been part of those celebrations for many years now. This year, I thought he would especially enjoy finding out if what we had been told, and also thought, would be confirmed. Or not! We sent him the kit about a month before his actual birthday and made plans for having a "reveal" party on his birthday. What a complete shock to find out how wrong we all were! It was all very exciting, and we certainly had a lot of fun with the new discovery.

As I mentioned, we adopted Paul just before his eleventh birthday. We have celebrated his "anniversary" of being a Gilmore almost every year. Paul has been grafted into our family and has taken on characteristics of being a Gilmore even though we do not share any DNA. We have taught him about what makes a good family, why family is important, what our family values are. Paul loves food, loves to cook, and loves to try new things. So do we! As his mom, I love to cook for him because I know he will enjoy whatever I make and will often want the recipe to try on his own. My husband, Glenn, worked with Paul and taught him how to build things and fix things around the house. Glenn also taught Paul how to take care of the car, change the oil, check the filters, and keep it clean. As a family, we all contributed to making our house a home and doing the necessary chores to make it a warm and lovely place not only for us but also for all of our friends and family. Our mantra was "First, we work, and then we play."

So learning to do chores and being disciplined would have a lasting impact on how he does life on his own. For example, when he first came to our house, he was a slob! His room was a mess; he took really long showers and didn't know how to keep himself or his room clean. We had to teach him these things. The upside was that he liked nice things! One of the first things he and I did together was to go to the fabric store and pick out material for curtains for his room. He had very definite ideas of what he liked, and I liked and affirmed his choices! He also liked to dress well. He still does! One of the things he still has a hard time with, though, is saving his money! If he had a few bucks, he wanted to spend it! That particular skill can take a lifetime to really learn!

I am also a stepparent. Our daughters Valerie and Marlena were ten and twelve when we got married. Becoming a stepparent as well as an adoptive parent certainly had challenges! But there have also been great times shared together! Navigating all of the various stages of growing up has given us all a deep appreciation and love for one another. Now that they are all grown and have families of their own, we rejoice that our grandchildren have also been brought up in the fear and admonition of the Lord (Ephesians 6:4).

This is a small representation of what happens when we become part of God's family. We are grafted into him. As we learn to live in him, we take on his likeness and characteristics. We want to share in all of the ways that being part of his family strengthens our ties to him.

So as adopted children learn the ways of their new family, so all believers in Jesus as Messiah will desire to grow and learn and live in the fullness of him. This would include doing the things that Jesus did while here on earth. The biblical feasts are expressions of the covenantal relationship that God has with his people. This includes those who believe in Jesus as Messiah! In each of the feasts and festivals, there are hints and clues that tell the story of God in its fullness. As we observe these feasts and festivals, we learn more about God, his Son Jesus Christ, and the workings of the Holy Spirit through history. We learn to see ourselves as part of that history and how we fit into God's divine purpose for all who believe.

This book is for those who want to learn more about being grafted into the roots of Jesus. Jesus was a Jew. His earthly DNA came from Jewish parentage. He did all the things that Jewish families of his day did. He studied Torah, worked with his earthly father Joseph, had friends, went to weddings, and journeyed with family and friends to Jerusalem for the yearly feasts and festivals—all the parts associated with being part of a Jewish community.

This book is also for those who want to learn more about celebrating the feasts and festivals of the Jewish year as well as the seasons of the church year and how they are all portraits of Christ our Messiah and can lead us into a deeper relationship with him. As you think about your own celebrations at home, consider your family first and how to include them.

If you are part of a church's hospitality team or a pastor, consider how to incorporate all the generations so that all feel included. Children can play an important part in each of the seasons! Their participation helps their spiritual formation as well by engaging them in activities, food preparation, readings, and storytelling! When the seasons, feasts, and festivals become a regular part of homelife and church life, we learn more about God, the biblical stories, faith, and enjoy sweet fellowship with others! Instilling and fostering the faith of a young child is one of the most important things a parent can do. There is also an added blessing as we recognize that people around the world are also coming together and doing the same. What I mean by this is that the church universally gathers for worship and engages in a variety of worship acts. Knowing that other churches around the world are praying, reading the same scriptures, worshiping the same God should cause us to feel connected with brothers and sisters in various denominations speaking many different languages yet knowing that God hears and sees all and accepts our worship! What an amazing thought! We are joining hands and hearts around the world in the glorious praise of our Messiah!

Are you ready? Let's dig in together!

CHAPTER 1

Why Is Any of This Important?

The Bible is God's story through which he has revealed his divine nature and how he desires to be worshiped. The biblical narrative takes the reader through the historical record of creation and the establishment of a special, chosen nation that would live in a unique covenant relationship with God. Through centuries of good and bad, God continued to reach out to his chosen nation through the giving of laws and commandments that would guide them in their lives and demonstrate to the nations around them that they served the one true God. When they became disobedient and rebellious and turned away from God and worshiped the gods of the surrounding nations, God sent judges, prophets, priests, and kings to remind them of the covenant of which they were a part and to lead them back into their service and devotion to him.

Because God is God, and there is none other, in his omniscience, he knew from the beginning that the people he created to live in community with him would break that covenant. So he set a plan in motion to bring about an ultimate restoration. He continued to show by blessing them with peace, fruitfulness, prosperity, and the promise of a savior that he would provide not only for his chosen people but also through them to all the people of the world.

William Dyrness, in his book *A Primer on Christian Worship*, says, "The beginning of worship is… God's invitation, given first in Israel, and then in Christ, to return to God, to be reconciled and healed. Thus the human practices of worship are responses to God's initiative… God approaches in invitation and blessing; we respond in faith."[4] Dr. Andrew Hill quotes Robert Shaper who defines worship "as the expression of a relationship in which God the Father reveals himself and his love in Christ and by his Holy Spirit administers grace, to which we respond in faith, gratitude, and obedience."[5] All of life then should be lived in response to God the Father who, with his Son and the Holy Spirit, created all there is for his own pleasure. The human response is to learn to know him more fully and live a life in such a way that honors and glorifies him (Psalm 149:4; Philippians 2:13).

The understanding of the events in the biblical history of the Israelite people—the law they were given, the festivals that were established, the symbols and actions that were involved—can lead to deeper level of knowing the Creator and his desire for his creation to know and worship him.

The feast and festivals were demonstrable ways to worship God and remember his covenant with his chosen people: Israel. These special commemorative seasons would point to God's intention to redeem and reconcile not only his chosen people but also all of humanity and thereby reestablish the community he originally created in the garden of Eden. Throughout biblical history, prophecy was fulfilled in Jesus Christ. The Old Testament prophecies regarding the Messiah, who would save and restore God's creation and mankind, can especially be seen in the events of the Exodus and the subsequent festivals. These historical events impact our worship today and must be understood in light of the culture and context in which they occurred.

---

4   William A. Dyrness, *A Primer on Christian Worship*. (Grand Rapids: William B. Eerdmans Publishing Company 2009), 2.
5   Andrew E. Hill, *Enter His Courts with Praise!* (Grand Rapids: Baker Books 1993), xix.

If worship "does God's story" as Robert Webber states,[6] what is God's story? God is timeless. He has no beginning and no end; therefore, his story really has no starting point. The history of creation has a starting point, and it is only at this point that we can begin to understand and tell "God's story."

If you grew up as I did, going to Sunday school and church, you are familiar with the biblical stories. I think it is important to review the stories as there is something new to be learned with each retelling. And as one reviews the stories, a new sense of God's faithfulness and trustworthiness is revealed.

The book of Genesis sets the stage and records God's creation of the heavens and the earth, night and day, the land and sea, plants and animals. It was created by his spoken word, and he proclaimed it "good." God then decided to make a man in his own image to take care of the world he created. Genesis 1:26 states, "Then God said, "Let Us make man in Our image, according to Our likeness…"[7] He created the world as a place that he and his creation (man) could live in community. He gave the man a home, Eden, to cultivate it and keep it (Genesis 2:15). God recognized that man did not have a partner, so he also created a woman. Genesis 3:8 records that "they heard the sound of the *Lord* God walking in the garden in the cool of the day…" God desired to meet with and have conversation with his creation. It was a perfect world and the perfect picture of relationship: God and humanity. It was also a picture of work.[8] God assigned his human creation the tasks of caring for the garden and naming the animals (Genesis 2:19). God gave man a purpose in carrying out these tasks. God also gave rules for living in the garden. Man was told he could eat of every tree except for one. At this point, man was given a choice. He could choose to obey the command or not.

---

6   Robert E. Webber, *Ancient-Future Worship* (Grand Rapids: Baker Books 2008), 29.

7   The use of the words *us* and *our* in this verse indicate that God is a Triune community. Webber states, "This Triune community is a person and is personal. The biblical and ancient definition of person is 'a being in community.'" Ibid., 31.

8   Ibid., 32.

When the serpent tempted Eve, she succumbed to the temptation and ate the fruit of the tree that was off-limits. She convinced Adam to also eat the fruit. When confronted by God of this breach, Adam passed the buck to Eve who passed the buck to the serpent. As a result, the perfect community was broken. Sin entered the world; God cursed the serpent and sent Adam and Eve out of the garden forever. The greatest result of this was death, and because of this sin, everything would be affected by it. All of creation would have a lifespan. What was to have been a perfect world where God and his creation could experience community was now turned into a desert where evil and death disrupted the life of every living thing. Yet God made a way for restoration of the community with his creation. The Old Testament records the trials and tribulations of God's chosen people and the often painful consequences of a broken covenant relationship. A brief review of that journey follows.

God called a man named Abram, from the land of Ur, along with his wife Sarai to leave their home and go to Canaan. God made a covenant with Abram that his offspring would become a great nation, and through him, all the nations of the earth would be blessed (Genesis 12). The "great nation" would become the nation of Israel. Abram, renamed Abraham, was promised a son, Isaac. Isaac had two sons; the younger, Jacob, had twelve sons. It was through these twelve that the nation of Israel took shape.

A great famine caused Jacob and his family to move to Egypt. At first, they were treated well. As time went by, a new Pharaoh came into power that knew nothing of the history of why or how the Israelites got there. He saw that they were prolific and lived in the best part of the country. He began to enslave the people so that they would not be able join forces with another kingdom and fight against the Egyptians (Exodus 1:10). During this time, Moses was born. Because of an edict that all Israelite baby boys should be killed, Moses's mother built a basket and placed him in the Nile River where the daughter of Pharaoh went to bathe. She found the basket and, in essence, adopted him. Because Moses's older sister Miriam was watching the basket, she offered to find a nurse for the child. His own mother nursed the child until he was old enough to go and live with Pharaoh's daughter.

When Moses became a man, he observed an Egyptian beating a Hebrew slave (Exodus 1:11). Moses killed the Egyptian and then ran to the desert of Midian because Pharaoh heard what he had done and tried to kill him (Exodus 1:15). Moses lived in the desert for forty years when God visited him in the form of a burning bush (Exodus 3:2). God told Moses to return to Egypt to lead the Israelites out of that land. This pivotal event set in motion a series of events that would demonstrate to the people of Israel that God had heard their cries for deliverance from their oppressors. When the people of Israel heard that God had heard their cries and had "seen their affliction, then they bowed low and worshiped" (Exodus 4:31).

Through numerous confrontations by Moses and his brother Aaron with Pharaoh to let the Israelites leave Egypt, God demonstrated his power by sending plagues all over the land. The tenth plague was death of the firstborn. God instructed the Israelites through Moses and Aaron that they were to prepare to leave the land of Goshen where they had lived for 430 years. As part of the preparation, they were to kill an unblemished lamb, smear its blood on the doorposts and lintel of their homes, then roast it, and eat it along with unleavened bread and bitter herbs (Exodus 12:7–8). The Angel of Death would then pass over the houses with the blood on the doorposts (verse 23). They were commanded to celebrate this event forever (verse 24). Moshe and Ceil Rosen state, "The nation of Israel needed a new beginning, a new birth. Thus the redemption at Passover prepared the sons of Jacob for another covenant to be made at Sinai, which would reestablish and reaffirm them as the nation of God." This event was the foreshadowing of what ultimately would be accomplished when Christ would come to die for the sin of mankind and offer a new covenant.

Webber states that Moses is a picture or symbol of Jesus. Moses was sent by God to deliver his people from their slavery in the desert. Christ was sent to deliver the world from the slavery of sin (Hebrews 3:1–6). The nation of Israel became a picture of the church. God dwelt with Israel in the desert in the tabernacle in the form of a cloud (Exodus 40:34) just as "the Word became flesh and dwelt among us" (John 1:14). The tabernacle foreshadowed the work of Jesus and the new covenant. It showed that hope was alive and would come from Israel in the Messiah who would bring restoration by reversing the effects of sin and restoring what had become a desert into God's garden of glory.[9]

Due to sins committed by the Israelite people, they had to wander in the wilderness for forty years. During that time, there continued to be grumbling and complaining against God for lack of food and the niceties of living conditions in Egypt. But God did supply their needs through miracles of manna, quail, and water (Exodus 16) and continued to lead them to the promised land.

God also continued to give directions for living and how to worship him. The books of Exodus and Leviticus record the laws given to the people through Moses and included specific directions for worship and religious festivals. Exodus 34 and Leviticus 23 describe what three of these festivals were, when they were to occur, and how they were to be celebrated. Each of the festivals had specific observances that included holy convocations or days of rest from work. The offerings, meals, and other parts of celebration were described in the books of Moses. Within these festival celebrations, one can see how God began to reveal his plan for redemption.

The first was Passover which was held in the first month, on the fourteenth day of the month at twilight (Leviticus 23:5). What immediately followed on the fifteenth day of the same month was the Feast of Unleavened Bread (verse 6). The second was Pentecost or Feast of Weeks, also known as the Feast of Firstfruits, was celebrated seven weeks after Passover (verse 16). The third was the Feast of Ingathering, also called the Feast of Tabernacles (Exodus 34:22). These three feasts coincided with harvest times in the yearly cycle. All three of these celebration times were to enable the Israelites to give thanks to God for supplying their physical needs and to acknowledge his presence in their lives. These three feasts "celebrate and actualize

---

[9] Ibid., 34.

the great threefold saving event in Israel's history: the Exodus, the Mosaic covenant, and the entrance into the promised land."[10]

All of the festivals were joyous occasions and focused on thanksgiving to the Creator, not the creation (Romans 1:25). These festivals set the Israelites apart from their Canaanite neighbors who worshiped many gods. The festivals were instituted so that the people of Israel would have a demonstrable way to live out the covenant that they made with God at Sinai and show to the nations around them that their God was God over all.[11] Each of the festivals was celebrated for seven days and had some elements in common such as presenting to the *Lord* various kinds of offerings and animal sacrifices.

Passover is the first night of the Feast of Unleavened Bread. On this night, the Seder meal is prepared and eaten. The story of being enslaved, bitterness and sorrow suffered at the hands of the Egyptians, and the exodus from Egypt is recounted as part of the meal. Blessings are said; four cups of wine are drunk, and children ask questions about why this celebration is important. Remembering and retelling are important parts of the celebration. The Seder meal consists of food that helps tell the story of the exodus. The exodus event set in motion a new beginning, or new birth, for the Israelites.[12] When the Israelites celebrated the first Passover in the desert, they sacrificed a lamb, roasted it, and ate it. They ate unleavened bread for seven days as well as bitter herbs to remind them of the harsh treatment they endured at the hands of the Egyptians. This was to be during the month of Nisan[13] (generally our month of April)—the month that the exodus occurred. They were not to do any work on the last

---

[10] Robert Webber, ed., *The Complete Library of Christian Worship*, Volume I, *The Biblical Foundations of Worship* (Nashville: Star Song Publishing Group, 1993), 181.

[11] David Brickner, *Christ in the Feast of Tabernacles* (Chicago: Moody Publishers, 2006), 24.

[12] Ceil and Moshe Rosen, *Christ in the Passover* (Chicago: Moody Publishers, 1987), 19.

[13] 13. Robert Webber, ed., *The Complete Library of Christian Worship*, Volume I, *The Biblical Foundations of Worship* (Nashville: Star Song Publishing Group, 1993), 191.

day of the festival as it was a "holy convocation" (Leviticus 23:8) and were to remember how God saved them from their oppressors and destroyed the firstborn of every household that was not covered by the blood of a sacrificed lamb. The point of this whole event was to bring about a way for there to be forgiveness for sins committed.

The lamb, the bitter herbs, the unleavened bread are all symbols that point to God's ultimate redemption plan. The leaven is a symbol for sin. Cleaning the house of all leaven and not eating anything with yeast is a representation of the child of God being transformed, or sanctified, by receiving forgiveness of sin." It is getting rid of the things in life that are a distraction from a relationship with God. Three pieces of unleavened bread, called matzo, referred to the affliction endured in Egypt. The middle piece was broken in half; one half was wrapped up in a napkin and hidden away. The three pieces have been said to represent the Patriarchs: Abraham, Isaac, and Jacob.[14] They also represent the Triune God. The middle *matzo,* the broken one, is a picture of the Messiah: a broken body, wrapped in a cloth, and buried.[15] The hidden piece was later "redeemed" at the end of the meal and brought back to the table for all to partake of one last piece. This symbolizes Christ's resurrection.[16] What was buried has been resurrected. Jesus referred to himself as the "bread of life." He also reminded the people that their "fathers ate manna in the wilderness and they died" (John 6:48, 49). If they would but partake of the living bread (verse 51), they would live forever. This reference was to the resurrection of the believers.

When Christ celebrated the Passover with his disciples, he pointed out to them what all the elements were designed to mean and his fulfillment of that meaning. He likened himself to the lamb: slain and blood shed so that sin would be forgiven. The unleavened bread was a picture of his body that would be pierced, beaten, and

---

[14] *The Messianic Passover Haggadah* (Baltimore, MD: The Lederer Foundation, 1989), 13.

[15] Coulson Shepherd, *Jewish Holy Days: Their Prophetic and Christian Significance* (Neptune, New Jersey: Loizeax Brothers, 1981), 27.

[16] Ibid., 28.

crucified (Isaiah 53). There would be no further need for animal sacrifice as he would be the ultimate, once and for all, sacrifice. Jesus was instituting a "new memorial. He was teaching the disciples in cryptic terms that after his death, the Paschal lamb would no longer have the same significance. It was the memorial of physical, historical redemption but only a shadow of the ultimate redemption soon to come" (Hebrews 9:14–15, 23–26).[17]

Pentecost was also called the Feast of Weeks because it occurred seven weeks or, more specifically, fifty days after Passover. It was the time for harvesting barley and was a wonderful celebration that included bringing two loaves of leavened bread and other free-will offerings to the *Lord* (Deuteronomy 16:10–11). Leviticus 23 describes the offerings that were to be brought to the priest to be presented before the *Lord*. A wave offering was made of a sheaf of grain from the firstfruits of the harvest (Leviticus 23:10). The priest would wave the grain before the *Lord* so that the presenter would be accepted (verse 11). Seven one-year-old male lambs, a bull, and two rams were also brought for sacrifice (verse 18) to the *Lord*. A male goat was brought for a sin offering and two lambs for a peace offering (verse 19).

Again, at this joyful celebration, meals were to be shared with strangers, widows, and Levites (Deuteronomy 16:11) as it was a time to rejoice and thank God for his blessing (verse 15). Hospitality was a reminder that they were once strangers in a land that was not their own. This was another symbolic reminder that the *Lord* had provided for the physical needs of his people.[18] In later tradition, the giving of the law at Sinai was included in this celebration (Exodus 19:1) as well as the reading of the book of Ruth, which describes the harvest. This practice contributed to the renewal of the covenant—remembering the Law that was given to the people through Moses in the desert.[19]

During Jesus's ministry, he took care of the physical needs of people through miraculous healings. He fulfilled the prophecy in

---

[17] Rosen. 58.

[18] Hill, 122.

[19] Ibid., 123.

Isaiah that said the Messiah "took our infirmities and carried away our diseases" (Isaiah 53:4, Matthew 8:17). He also miraculously fed thousands of people on more than one occasion that had come to hear him teach (Matthew 14–15, Mark 6, 8, John 6). In Matthew 25:32–40, Jesus told his disciples of the coming judgment and who would inherit the kingdom. Regarding how they treated others, Jesus told them, "Truly I say to you, to the extent that you did to one of these brothers of mine, even to the least of them, you did it to me." In the book of Acts, new believers devoted themselves not only to the apostles "teaching and to fellowship but to the breaking of bread and to prayer…and were sharing with all as anyone might have need" (Acts 2:42–45). The Apostle Paul also exhorted the Roman believers to continue to practice hospitality (Romans 12:13).

The prophetic fulfillment of this festival was seen in the day of Pentecost, fifty days after Jesus's resurrection, when the Holy Spirit was poured out on the disciples that were gathered in the Upper Room (Acts 2:1–3). The church was born that day when the Spirit came to unite the believers into "one loaf or body."[20] In the book of Acts chapter 2, the apostle Peter gave an account of how Jesus fulfilled the prophecies of Joel and King David. Pentecost points to Christ as the head of the church that came into existence that day. "The Holy Spirit united the believers in that body and, since then, all true Jewish and Gentile believers are not only indwelt by the Holy Spirit but are baptized into that same body."[21]

The Feast of Ingathering, also known as Booths or Tabernacles, was to celebrate the fall harvest of fruits, olives, and wine grapes. This festival occurred in the month of Tishri, late September or early October.[22] The people were to set up temporary shelters, or booths, to live in for a week. These mini tabernacles were made of fruits, palm fronds, leafy branches, and willows (Leviticus 23:40). The Talmud gives instruction on how to build a *sukkah* or booth. It was decorated with various kinds of fruits and structured so that the sky

---

[20] Shepherd, 54.
[21] Ibid., 55.
[22] Webber, 191.

could be seen through the roof.[23] This was a reminder of the tents they lived in while wandering in the desert. On the first day of the festival, a wave offering was offered to God. Joining together a palm branch with a myrtle branch and a willow branch is called a *Lulav*. A *lulav* was combined with a piece of citrus fruit called an *etrog*. The *lulav* and etrog were held with both hands and shaken. Tradition says that these were waved, or shaken,[24] in six directions—north, east, south, west, up, and down—as the Hallel Psalms (Psalms 118–121) were recited. "The rabbis taught that the citron represented the heart of human beings, while the palm branch corresponded to the spine, the myrtle to the eyes, and the willow to the mouth. Thus the *lulav* and etrog became a symbol of the bodily dedication to God."[25] This offering was brought on the first day of the week. The sheaf represented the harvest. Christ was resurrected on the first day of the week and is referred to as the "firstfruits" in 1 Corinthians 15:16–23.[26] Christ fulfilled the promise that those who believed would be raised from the dead (Leviticus 23:10) and will be raised up at his coming again (1 Thessalonians 4:13–18; 1 Corinthians 15:23, 51–57).[27]

In later times, a water-pouring ceremony was added to the festival.[28] Water was obviously necessary for the crops to grow, so God was invoked to send rain so that there would be fruitful harvests. On the last day of the Feast of Tabernacles, Jesus appealed to people's spiritual thirst and invited, "If any man is thirsty, let him come to me and drink" (John 7:37). On another occasion, Jesus told a Samaritan woman that he could give her living water so that she would thirst no more (John 4:10, 14).

Also during this festival, it was considered charitable, a *mitzvah*, to invite a less fortunate person or a stranger to share a meal. The apostle Paul exhorted believers to present their bodies as a "living and holy sacrifice, acceptable to God, which is your spiritual service

---

[23] 23.Brickner, 54.
[24] Ibid., 55.
[25] Ibid., 56.
[26] Shepherd, 33.
[27] Ibid., 37.
[28] Brickner, 78.

of worship" (Romans 12:1). The four species of the festival can also be likened to the fruit of the Spirit mentioned in Galatians 5:22. Brickner states that if we exhibit the fruit of the Spirit in our lives, we "figuratively shake it up and wave it before God. He is the One who should get the glory from the fruit that he has put in our lives."[29]

"Ingathering" prophetically refers to the ingathering of all the nations that will occur in the new millennium. Zechariah 14:8–16 describes how the feast will be celebrated in Jerusalem and that the remnant of the nations will go to worship there. During this time, the nation of Israel will acknowledge its mistake of not recognizing the Messiah when he came the first time and died for sins but will, at this future time, call upon him (Zechariah 13:9).[30]

The rest of the story that is told throughout the Old Testament is preparation for the coming of the Messiah. This was the record of how God continued to reach out to his people in order to bring them to reconciliation with himself, which is the greatest demonstration of love.[31] The story of the New Testament is that he is coming again and with the second coming will finally bring about the full restoration of his creation. Webber calls this the "garden of reversal…the sin of the first-formed man is amended by the second Adam [Christ]."[32] Through the death of Jesus on the cross, he paid the price for all humanity's sin and made a way for all to be reconciled to him (John 3:16). The full restoration of his creation will be when evil is dispelled, and Christ comes again to reign in glory and majesty upon the earth (Revelation 21).

Probably the most difficult thing for a finite mind to understand is that God became flesh. This is the mystery of the incarnation (John 1:14). Again Webber states parenthetically that "there really are no words that fully describe the mystery of this union [God and man]."[33] This is the majesty and mystery of God together demon-

---

[29] Ibid., 58.
[30] Shepherd, 78.
[31] Webber, 81.
[32] *Ancient-Future Worship* (Grand Rapids: Baker Books 2008), 34.
[33] Ibid., 38.

strated to all mankind his divine nature and supremacy over evil and death (Colossians 2:15). It is because of this that we are compelled by the Holy Spirit to worship this God who yearns to have fellowship with us and ultimately will bring about full restoration of his creation. Until the day that Christ returns, those who profess Christ as Lord and Savior are to tell the world of God's redeeming love and proclaim the hope that we have in him for the coming world (Matthew 28:19–20). Those who have trusted in Christ for salvation become one with him and are members of his body: the church. Webber most succinctly states, "The full story is that of the work of the Father, the Son, and the Holy Spirit. God creates, becomes involved with creation, and is made incarnate into time, space, and history in order to redeem and restore the world as the garden of God's habitation and people as his community of love and fellowship."[34]

In summary, God's divine nature and character can be seen through his acts of creation, the establishment of a chosen people, the giving of laws, and the making of a covenant to live exclusively in a relationship with him. God called his people to respond to his leading and desire to follow and worship him alone. Some chose to follow; others rejected him. Through the biblical festivals, the signs and symbols clearly point to Jesus, the Messiah, and his mission. For me personally, having this historical record to read and study continues to compel me to believe and desire to follow and worship him. It is a daily offering that I give myself to him in sacrifice and worship. It compels me to desire to worship in a community that also believes and desires to live a life that honors him. These specific festivals that have been very briefly described here continue to give me insight into his divine nature and character and cause me to give thanks for the greatest gift given in Jesus, the Messiah, especially as I partake of and participate in the Lord's Supper.

As I continue to read and study, I am overwhelmed by his awesome power, his indescribable love, and how it draws me to him. I would affirm that worship, "prayer, praise, testimony, and so on is an end in itself; this end is part of a larger goal: that all of life, in whole

---

[34] Ibid., 43.

and in part (including the part we call worship), should serve and reflect God's glory."[35] As I go about my own daily tasks, I am even more aware of his presence in my life. This also compels me to intentionally order my life in such a way that it brings glory and honor to him. Just as in biblical times God continues to invite me into communion with him, I must accept the invitation daily and faithfully.

---

[35] William A. Dyrness, *A Primer on Christian Worship* (Grand Rapids: William B. Eerdmans Publishing Company 2009), 49.

Crown-shaped challah bread

Rosh Hashanah centerpiece

Table Décor, Rosh Hashanah

CHAPTER 2

The Year Begins: Rosh Hashanah, Yom Kippur

In the beginning, You laid the foundation of the earth and set the skies above us with Your own hands. But while they will someday pass away, You remain forever; when they wear out like old clothes, You will roll them up and change them into something new, and they will pass away.
—*Psalm 139:25–26*

Civic Calendar: Labor Day—September
Biblical Calendar: Rosh Hashanah, Yom Kippur—September/October

Since most Americans can relate to the start of the school year being in either late August or early September, that's where we will begin.

If your family includes children of any school age, you may be taking a family vacation during the summer months. You may also be preparing for the next school year by shopping for new clothes and purchasing school supplies. These days, stores are advertising school supplies as early as June! Getting ready for school is certainly a big deal and important part of family life.

Churches also, typically, will have some sort of fall kickoff. It might be the first Sunday of September, which could include a Labor Day celebration. Most colleges and universities begin classes the day after Labor Day. So this is a good time to think about new beginnings.

As parents and grandparents, we have a special obligation to instill in our children and grandchildren the precepts of the faith. They may not just "catch it," they need to be "taught" it. An excellent example of this imperative comes from a video series that our Sunday school class watched many years ago. It was titled *The Three Chairs: Experiencing Spiritual Breakthroughs* by Bruce Wilkinson. In the video, he gave this description of how faith is passed on in the example of Joshua. He used the metaphor of three chairs as representing three generations. In the first chair was Joshua—a person of commitment who had experienced the works of God; he wanted to serve God so that God would be honored. In the second chair were the elders of Israel who had seen the works of God but did not experience them in the same way (Joshua 24:14–15, 31). In the third chair were those who did not know the works of God (Judges 2:7, 10) because their parents may have stopped telling the stories, and so they had no personal stories to tell.[36] The first chair represented the person who has a vital relationship with God. The second chair represented those who were raised in a firsthand family of faith and had the benefits of parental teaching but for some reason did not choose to stay close to God. The third chair represented those who rejected God or moved far away from him in order to focus on themselves. This pattern continued throughout the Old Testament. Some kings who chose to follow God and listened to the prophets were blessed. Those who did not know God led the people astray and were punished.

So right from the start, I want to implore pastors, parents, grandparents, and all those who work with children in church to be even more intentional about including young ones of all ages into the planning, preparation, and execution of the feasts and celebrations.

The Jewish calendar has several "firsts." This can sound confusing, so here is a quick explanation: Tishri (first of September) is

---

[36] Bruce Wilkinson, *The Three Chairs: Experiencing Spiritual Breakthroughs* (Atlanta, Georgia: Walk Through the Bible Ministries, 2000) from notes I found in my Bible and an email conversation with a friend (dated April 3, 2012) who showed the video series in our Sunday school class in 1998.

Rosh Hashanah; Feast of Trumpets is the new year for years; Shevat 15 (February) is the new year for trees and firstfruits; Nisan (first of March or April) is the new year for the coronation of the king; and Elul (first of August) is the new year for tithing of animals.

The Jewish feast of *Rosh Hashanah* is a day of new beginning. It is the Jewish New Year, and it is a time for great celebration! Rosh Hashanah actually means "Head of the Year." *L'shana tova* is the greeting which means "a good year." *Shana tovah u'metukah'* means "a good sweet year." Much like the western calendar's New Year's Day on January 1, Rosh Hashanah is the beginning of the Jewish New Year. But there is much more to it than the date change, parties, and celebrations and New Year resolutions. *Rosh Hashanah* has some of those elements, but it has so much more! It is considered by the ancients to be the day that God created the universe and Adam and Eve. It is celebrated with lighting candles in the evening, blowing the *shofar,* a ram's horn, and enjoying festive meals with family and friends. It is also a time for reflection, looking back on the past year, and looking forward to the New Year.

In many ways, it is like a time of rededication to the things that are important, primarily checking our relationship with God, and how we have grown spiritually and how we can continue in our faith journey. Observant Jews will celebrate *Yom Kippur* ten days after *Rosh Hashanah* as a day of remembrance and a day of judgment. Many prayers will be said asking God to grant a year of peace, prosperity, and blessing. In the recited prayers, it states that on this day, "all inhabits of the world pass before God like a flock of sheep,"[37] and it is decreed in the heavenly court "who shall live, and who shall die... who shall be impoverished and who all be enriched, who shall fall and who shall rise[38]."

For believers in Jesus, Messiah, the day recalls our own salvation and reminds us of our brokenness and need for forgiveness. Much like when we come to the Lord's Table, we first ask for forgiveness of

---

[37] https://jewishweek.timesofisrael.com/counting-sheep-on-rosh-hashanah/. (Accessed 9/23/2020).

[38] Ibid.

our sins, and then we rejoice in being forgiven and give thanks for all that Jesus, the Messiah, has done for us.

Observant Jews will blow a *shofar* many times during the celebrations. The blowing of the *shofar* represents the trumpet blasts as at a king's coronation. It is also a call to repentance. The *shofar* proclaims the kingship of God. It reminds us to examine ourselves, confess our sin, and ask for God to lead and guide us in the New Year. Blowing the *shofar* also reminds us that it was blown at the giving of the Torah at Mt. Sinai as well as recalling the message of the prophets who later called the children of God to repentance and follow his commandments. It reminds us of the destruction of the physical temple and helps us focus on the temple of our bodies that the Messiah indwells. It reminds us of the faith that Abraham had in offering his son Isaac as a sacrifice and how this was a foreshadowing of what Jesus, our Messiah, would do by offering himself up for us as our sacrifice. The blowing of the *shofar* reminds us of the sovereignty of God and how much he loves us, his creation.

Blowing the *shofar* is also a sign of the return of Christ, our Messiah. The Jews of Jesus's day were looking for a warrior to come and rescue them from the Romans. Jesus, our Messiah, came first to save his people from their inner selves and their sin. He will come again as Ruler and King, and we are to be prepared.

As in all feasts and festivals, there are many things to consider and focus on. As you learn more about each one, you will decide what to emphasize depending on the needs and desires of your family. We typically plan our celebrations around who will be coming. I try to get commitments from family first, and then invite some friends to also join us. This year we included having family from across the country join in by Zoom. What fun it was to see them and also have them participate in reading the blessings! I had emailed the liturgy ahead of time so that they could have it in hand.

Okay, let's get down to the good stuff! What are some ways to begin to celebrate these important events? As in any event, preparation is often key to success! So as you are preparing for the beginning of a school year and other fall events, think of it in terms of the New Year,

Rosh Hashanah, and new beginnings. New beginnings mean reflecting on the past year first, what was good, what was accomplished, how did you grow as a person? Also, be honest and reflect on what was not good. How can not-so-good things be rectified or turned into good things? *Rosh Hashanah* is also about forward thinking and the resolve to make things right and do better. If you are list-maker personality, then perhaps writing down your reflections can help. If you are more verbal, perhaps sharing around the dinner table is a good way to reflect, and as others hear your thoughts, you can all help hold each other accountable for the coming year. A general practice that our eldest daughter and son-in-law have done with their four children is to go around the table before dinner, and each one tells one good thing and one not-so-good thing that happened that day. I think this is a great way to get your kids to talk about themselves and for parents to find out what is going on in their heads! Especially as they become teenagers!

Confession and reconciliation are good things and can be most meaningful. Give thanks for all the blessings that you have received as well! You can even make it fun!

With all that in mind, let's get ready for the celebration. It's a new year, so let the festivities begin! The main themes for this feast are the following: (1) celebrating the creation of the world, (2) the royalty of God, (3) remembrance, and (4) judgment. You may want to use just one of these themes for your celebration. Everything means something, so choose your menu items and decorations and even prayers or things you want to say so that they reflect the spirit of the celebration and God who gives good things to his children and desires to bless them.

Menu Ideas

Foods that are appropriate and reflect the special day: apples, honey, pomegranates, and dates. Sweet foods are representative of a sweet new year. Eating the fruits that are new to this season is also significant and representative of our gratefulness for the life we enjoy. Challah bread, shaped into a circle or spiral, symbolize continuity.

Challah is often dipped in honey before eating and shared around the table.

Fish is often used as a main course. You may not want to use a whole fish as some might think it's gross to have a whole fish staring from a plate! But the symbolism of the whole fish is that this is the head of the New Year, and the head of the fish reminds us of that! You could use a fake whole fish as part of a centerpiece to symbolize the head of the New Year!

If you are not into fish, try chicken. Chicken is quite often easier to prepare and not as daunting as other meats might be. Try a sweet kind of marinade either prepared or mixed from scratch!

Side dishes

Couscous is considered a savory dish and is a great option for incorporating vegetables. Couscous is made up of a myriad of little beads and represents the many blessings you hope to receive this next year. Vegetables such as carrots, leeks, and spinach can be easy to prepare.

Dessert

Apple-honey cake is a great dessert and can be made in a variety of ways. You can include walnuts or dates and use spices such as cinnamon, cloves, nutmeg, and allspice. Some variations on the recipe might also include rum! Doesn't that sound divine?

Decorations and table setting

I like to find excuses for using my best dishes. I would set my table with my grandmother's china, use the silver flatware and crystal stemware. Nothing says you have to be uber-fancy; use whatever you have. Make it all look festive! I choose earth tones for a tablecloth and napkins.

For a centerpiece, I would build a tower of real fruits in a large bowl. Using pomegranates and apples as the base and then adding dates and nuts (in shells) for texture. Candles are also appropriate as they add warmth and light.

If your focus will be on the creation of the world, use a small globe as a centerpiece with a piece of blue/green cloth underneath to represent water. A few small toy fish could also be strewn around the base. Spread out some cotton batting to represent clouds. Add some birds and fish onto the cloth and batting for added effect!

For an emphasis on coronation, using a *shofar* (ram's horn) is significant. The blowing of the *shofar* signifies the coming of the King of kings! Psalm 98:6 says, "With trumpets and the sound of the horn shout joyfully before the King, the *Lord*." Jewish tradition says that the day God created the world, he also sat in judgment. Genesis 1:31 states that after all God created, he determined "it was very good." Use small horns and trumpets in your table decor to emphasize this theme. You could even make a crown for the center of your table to reflect the coming King!

If you have young children at your dinner, invite them to share what they expect to learn this next year and what they may anticipate. Adults can also share, briefly, reflections from the past year and hopes for the New Year. As you light candles and bless the meal, give thanks to God for all his many blessings and for his grace to abide over all. Ask him for forgiveness for wrongs done and a clean heart and renewed spirit. Incorporate Psalm 51 into your prayer. This part of your liturgy could be written, and you could all say the prayer responsively. This is an example of a responsive prayer:

> LEADER. Blessed are you, O God, King of the universe! You have blessed us through this past year, and we are thankful for your graciousness to us.
>
> ALL. God of all glory, on this first day of creation, bringing light out of darkness, On this first day, you began your new creation, raising Jesus Christ out of the darkness of death.

LEADER. On this day, grant that we, the people you created by water and the Spirit, may be joined with all your world in praising you for your great glory. Amen.[39]

See appendix 2 for the full liturgy.

Writing your own prayer, using some scripture, can help everyone focus and feel included in offering thanks to God. Use language that is appropriate for all at your table. Don't be concerned with "high and lofty" sounding verbiage! Make it meaningful to you! God will honor the prayers from your heart.

Is there any other God like You, who forgives evil and passes over the transgressions done by Yours who remain? He does not hold onto His anger forever because He delights in showing love and kindness. He will take pity on us again, will tread our wrongdoing underfoot. He will cast all our sins down to the bottom of the sea. (Micah 7:18–19)

These verses allude to the mercy of God. We ask for his mercy even as we ask for his forgiveness for wrongdoing.

Some Extras

According to Jewish tradition, the following happened on Tishri 1:

- Creation of the world
- The flood was dried up
- Enoch was taken by God (Genesis 5:24)

---

[39] The Worship Sourcebook (Grand Rapids: The Calvin Institute of Christian Worship; Faith Alive Christian Resources; Baker Books), 69.

- Sarah, Rachel, and Hannah conceived (1 Samuel 1)
- Joseph freed from the Egyptian prison by Pharaoh
- Job contracted leprosy
- Restart of sacrifices on the altar built by Ezra (Ezra 3:3)

Yom Kippur is the Day of Atonement in the Jewish calendar. It happens on Tishri 10. I have combined most of the elements of this day in the *Rosh Hashanah* celebration in an effort to simplify things for our family! Here are a few more thoughts about this very special day. The Day of Atonement commemorates the confession of sin and receiving forgiveness. In Jewish custom, it is a day of fasting, prayer, and repentance both personally and nationally.

The Day of Atonement is a reminder that the sacrifices made on the Altar of Burnt Offering were not enough to atone for sin (Leviticus 23:27). Leviticus 16:21–22 describes,

> Aaron will place both his hands on the goat's head and confess aloud over it all the guilt, rebellion, and wrongdoings of the people of Israel. In this way, he will transfer the sins of the people onto the goat's head; then another man who has been selected for this special task will drive the goat into the wilderness. When the man releases the goat into the desert, it will carry all the offenses of God's people away into the desolate wastelands.

Jesus came to fulfill this action that Aaron demonstrated (Hebrews 7:26–28).

> It is only fitting that we should have a High Priest who is devoted to God, blameless, pure, compassionate toward but separate from sinners, and exalted by God to the highest place of honor. Unlike other high priests, He does not

first need to make atonement every day for His own sins, and only then for His people's, because He already made atonement, reconciling us with God once and forever when He offered Himself as a sacrifice. The law made imperfect men high priests; but after that law was given, God swore an oath that made His perfected Son a high priest for all time.

Have you heard the expression, "Confession is good for the soul?" It is true. Confession is hard but necessary. Giving and receiving forgiveness can also be difficult. We try to teach our children about telling the truth when they have done something wrong. We also want them to ask for forgiveness, and we offer forgiveness to them. God also wants to hear us ask him for forgiveness of our sins. "But if we own up to our sins, God shows that He is faithful and just by forgiving us of our sins and purifying us from the pollution of all the bad things we have done" (1 John 1:9). What joy and relief it is to know that he does forgive us and "as far as the east is from the west, he remembers our sin no more" (Psalm 103:12).

CHAPTER 3

Sukkot: The Feast of Tabernacles

*I want you to do this so that all present and future generations of your
people remember that I sheltered the Israelites in booths like these
after I led them out of Egypt. I am the Eternal One, your God.*
—Leviticus 23:43

*Abundance of joys are in Your presence, eternal
pleasures at Your right hand.*
—Psalm 16:11

The Lord has done great things for us and we are glad.
—Psalm 126:3

Church Calendar: Reformation Sunday, All Saints Day—October
Biblical Calendar: Sukkot and Simchat Torah—September/October

"God set up the Feast of Tabernacles so that Israel, among other
things, would be reminded annually of his provision of a harvest that
supplied the food for the rest of the year."[40] For us today, it is still
a reminder of his goodness and daily provision for us as well as his
presence with us. In this season of our lives, I am thankful for a roof

---

[40] David Brickner, *Christ in the Feast of Tabernacles* (Chicago: Moody Publishers,
2006), 21.

over my head and a refrigerator that is mostly full, an extra freezer, and a small pantry that I try to keep well-stocked! I am also thankful and grateful that God is ever-present with me!

Ancient civilizations all had some kind of harvest festivals. God established this particular feast for the Israelites so that they would understand the seasons of life. He wanted them to know him as Creator and Provider and to worship him—not the creation but the Creator, not the provisions but the Provider. Interestingly, the Pilgrims that came to America knew about this feast, and the American Thanksgiving was possibly founded upon this festival. "Before coming to the New World, the Pilgrims lived for a short time among Sephardic Jews in Holland."[41] The Pilgrims would have observed the Sephardic Jews, who had come from Spain, as they celebrated this special feast. Interestingly, the cornucopia is shaped somewhat like a *shofar* which was blown on Yom Kippur. The Pilgrims shared a thanksgiving meal with their Indian friends who had helped them learn to plant corn and catch fish.

Another important aspect of Ingathering is how it connects the people to the land. God's people were to be forever linked with the land that he promised to give them—a land filled with milk and honey (Exodus 3:8).

The feast has four names, and sometimes, it is easy to get confused about which feast is being referred to! In Hebrew, names are very significant. Each of these names helps us understand the importance and significance of the feast.

Ha-Hag or the Feast is a reference to this feast as *the* feast. Unlike the others, this is the big one! It was the biggest event of the year! Solomon dedicated the temple during this feast. The feast relates to dancing and celebration, ceremonial procession and parties into the night! This is the last of the three pilgrim feasts where the people of Israel were to journey to Jerusalem. The Bible tells us that these festivals were to be in Jerusalem. The journey to be with God in

---

[41] https://toriavey.com/toris-kitchen/sukkot-the-harvest-holiday/ (accessed 9/23/2020).

his holy place was central to the feast. "True worship of God always involves a journey."[42]

The season of rejoicing comes from Jewish tradition. It is implied in Deuteronomy 16:13–15. "And you shall *rejoice* in your feast…" The word *rejoice* is mentioned several times in this passage. It is not used in reference to Passover and only once in reference to Pentecost.

There are lots of events in our lives that cause us to rejoice. This spiritual celebration also is a time for rejoicing in God's goodness. God wanted his people to be in relationship with him in a spirit of joyfulness. Unlike their neighbors who served gods that they were fearful of, the Israelites were to experience God in all his fullness and find joy in being in his presence and in serving him.

Sukkot, or Tabernacles, is the name most used to denote this festival. It recalls how the Israelites lived in tents during their time in the wilderness. After they moved into the promised land, they were to build tents and live in them for seven days (Leviticus 23) so that their children, and all following generations, would remember that they lived in tents when God brought them out of the land of Egypt.

God promised to give his children a land that flowed with milk and honey. The promise was that they would be blessed in their new homeland. But once a year, they were to remember how they got there and their dependence on God to guide and provide for them.

God provided for his children by giving them his presence. In the wilderness, God showed himself in a pillar of fire at night and a cloud during the day. After they built the Tabernacle, God's presence rested over the Tabernacle. He was demonstrating to them, and to us, that he is *with* us at all times. The Tabernacle was a temporary place. The sacrifices, burning incense, the ark of the covenant, and priestly worship were a constant reminder of God's holy presence. It was placed in the middle of the camp so that all the people could see it and have access to it.

God still desires to "tabernacle" with his people. Sukkot is about rejoicing over God's *past* provision, God's *current* provision, his faith-

---

[42] Brickner, 29.

fulness, atonement, presence with his people, and *promise* of our eternal home.

Sukkot is about rejoicing! It celebrates the gift of God's presence now and for eternity when our joy will be made full. So let's celebrate!

See appendix 2 for liturgy for *Sukkot*.

Menu Ideas

This is a wonderful time to celebrate with guests and family. As the season changes and fall foods become available, it is a great time to change up the menu and plan some wonderful dishes for a meal to be shared! There aren't any Sukkot-only dishes that I have found but many variations on other dishes that can be made and served. If a dish was a really good one for one meal, why not for another? Challah bread can be made with whole wheat flour for this occasion. It should be dipped in honey and broken into large pieces and served. A mixed green salad with beets and walnuts is a tasty first course. If the weather has cooled off, a butternut and apple soup make for a warm and welcome change. *Tzimmes* or orange-glazed carrots are a delicious side to go with brisket or meatballs with mushroom sauce. Finish off your meal with almond cookies or a fruit tart or strudel.

Decorating Ideas

The four species are made up of four different kinds of plants (citron/etrog, palm/*lulav*, myrtle/hadas, and palm/arava).[43] They are bound together to form what is called a *lulav*. Waving the *lulav* (literally) and saying a blessing over them is considered a *mitzvah* (good deed). A *lulav* can be used as the focal point in a centerpiece. Since this festival comes at the onset of fall, now is the time to get out your fall decorations! Use fall fruits and flowers in wreaths, table centerpieces, and wall décor.

---

[43] https://www.myjewishlearning.com/article/celebrating-sukkot-without-a-sukkah/. (Accessed 9/16/2020).

Lulav decor for *Sukkot* includes the four species

Chicken shwarma salad with pita wedges for *Sukkot*

Rosh Hashanah décor with *shofar*

CHAPTER 4

Advent, Hanukkah and the Christmas Season

*On another occasion, Jesus spoke to the crowds again. Jesus: I am the
light that shines through the cosmos; if you walk with Me, you will
thrive in the nourishing light that gives life and will not know darkness.
—John 8:12*

Civic Calendar: Veteran's Day, Thanksgiving—November
Church Calendar: Christ the King Sunday—November
Advent: November/December
Christmas, Christmastide: December 25–January 5
Biblical Festival: Hanukkah—December

J ust as the Jewish year is beginning, the seasons of the Christian
year are coming to a close! The Christian year, or church year, begins
with Advent. If we lay out the calendars month by month, we can see
where everything falls and how feasts and seasons will overlap.

September/October
Biblical feasts: Rosh Hashanah, Yom Kippur, Sukkot
Church year: Ordinary time
October
Church year: Reformation Sunday, All Saints Day
November

Church year: Christ the King Sunday (end of Ordinary time)
December
Biblical feast: Hanukkah
Church year: Advent, Christmas, Christmastide, 12 days of Christmas
January
Church year: Epiphany, Ordinary time

The timing of *Hanukkah* and Christmas, most years, is a real challenge. A couple of years ago, *Hanukkah* landed the first week of December! It was perfect as I could decorate for *Hanukkah* and focus on just that. Then, when it was over, move on to Advent and Christmas. That schedule doesn't happen very often. This past year, *Hanukkah* began a few days before Christmas and ended a couple days after Christmas. What to do with all the decorations and food choices? To top it all off, Advent begins the Sunday after Thanksgiving, and I almost always feel like I am slamming into the season full tilt! This means that I typically will get my Christmas decorations out the Saturday after Thanksgiving. My anniversary also happens during the week of Thanksgiving, just to complicated things all the more!

Just as most families have to juggle birthdays, anniversaries, holidays, and whatever else is important in their lives, so it is with spiritual seasons. I think what it comes down to is how to prioritize, plan, and execute. And the beauty of it all is seeing how all of these feasts and seasons complement, enhance, and give significance to our lives as we strive to honor God.

What is *Hanukkah*? *Hanukkah* is not one of the original feasts that God commanded the Israelites to celebrate as found in Leviticus 23. But it was important enough historically that it is mentioned in the book of John, and Jesus celebrated it also. John 10:22 states, "At that time the Feast of the Dedication took place at Jerusalem; it was winter, and Jesus was walking in the temple in the portico of Solomon." It is a matter-of-fact mention of the time of year and what was happening. It gives context to what Jesus was doing and where he was.

Hanukkah is the Festival of Light or Dedication. The history of *Hanukkah* goes back to the time when the Syrian-Greeks ruled in Jerusalem. It was the Hellenistic era, and the Greeks wanted everyone to adopt their worldview. Antiochus IV was a bad guy, and he tried to force the Jews to practice idolatry. Some Jews assimilated, but others did not and died as martyrs. Antiochus erected statues of Zeus in the temple and even sacrificed a pig on the altar. This was the last straw for a small band of men known as the Maccabees. Under the leadership of Judah, the Maccabee, a small band of his brothers, and others revolted against the Greeks. There was also a woman, named Judith, who was instrumental in killing a Syrian-Greek general. She is hailed as a hero among women in Jewish history. That act also helped to defeat the army. The Maccabees were eventually successful against the strong Syrian-Greek army, drove them out of Jerusalem, and declared their independence. When they went in to the temple to clean and repair it, they found there was only enough purified oil to light the six-foot menorah for one night. They knew that God had commanded that the menorah must always be lit. Now the oil that was to be used in lighting the menorah had to be purified (made kosher). They found enough oil to last for one night only! Not wanting to wait, they lit the menorah and illuminated the holy place. Miraculously, the oil lasted for eight days! This gave enough time for more oil to be made and delivered to the temple. There is much more to this story, and if you are interested, you can do your own research to read more about it! The story can be found in the first and second book of Maccabees. From a historical perspective, the event is important as it portrays the story of Jewish independence and resolve to stand up for their beliefs. The Greeks were ultimately working to destroy the Jews by destroying their values, belief in God, and way of life. "The Jews of the time objected to the Greek philosophy of being separate from God [they] realized that without a clear objective basis for morality, Greek literature and philosophy was of little value, because without God's guiding hand and commandments, philosophy could justify any cruelty."[44]

---

[44] Doron Kornbluth, *The Jewish Holiday Handbook* (Mosaica Press, 2014), 68.

Judah Maccabee was hailed as a savior. He was not *the* Messiah, but his courage and bravery led others to stand up for what was right. The continuity of the Jewish community and home was preserved because of his valor. Today, the celebration of *Hanukkah* centers on the home as well as the community. Can you even imagine what life would be like without traditions? What if all our traditions were against the law?

Celebrating Hanukkah

In our house, whenever the dates for *Hanukkah* fall, planning begins as soon as Thanksgiving is over if not before. As I mentioned earlier, I haul out the decorations the Saturday after Thanksgiving. (Remember the first Sunday of Advent is the next day.)

Decorations for Hanukkah

Decorations for *Hanukkah* includes a nine-branch menorah and thirty-nine candles, *gelt* (gold chocolate coins), and *dreidels* (little spinning tops). Why so many candles? The *shammash* is lit every night. *Shammash* means "servant." It is the servant candle that lights all the other candles. Do you see the underlying meaning for this? The servant candle represents the Messiah, the Servant of all. Each night, light the *shammash* and one more candle. There is an order to lighting the candles. The *shammash* is always lit first and then used to light the other candles. On my menorah, the tallest candles is on the far right when looking at it. So I light the *shammash* and then use it to light the candle farthest to the left. On remaining nights, light the *shammash* then candles from left to right adding a new candle each night. The candles should be allowed to burn all the way out and not blown Out. This is why you will need thirty-nine candles! In a Jewish home, the menorah will be lit by the front door as a reminder that the door is the "gateway to Jewish family life."[45] The window at the front of my house does not have a very wide ledge, so typically, I do not put a menorah in the front window. Someday, I may figure out a way to have one there! Colors for this season are typically blue and white. You can add silver and gold as beautiful accents!

Menorah

If you do not have a *Hanukkah* menorah, you can craft one with eight candleholders or votives that are all the same height. You will also need one that is higher than all the others. The tallest one will be your *shammash*. The candles should be placed in a straight row. This can make for a lovely centerpiece! Before lighting the candles, recite the blessing. There are three blessings. On the first night, recite all three. The second through eighth nights, recite blessings one and two. If you have children, let them take turns reciting the blessing. After lighting the correct number of candles each night, let them stay lit for at least half an hour.

Blessing 1. Blessed are You, Lord our God, King of the universe, who has sanctified us with His commandments and commanded us to kindle the *Hanukkah* light.

Blessing 2. Blessed are You, Lord our God, King of the universe, who performed miracles for our forefathers in those days at this time.

Blessing 3. Blessed are You, Lord our God, King of the universe, who has granted us life, sustained us, and enabled us to reach this occasion.

Lighting the candles and reading scripture are part of the celebration of *Hanukkah*. Each night, there is a prayer and a reading. This can be done before dinner or after. Children will love to play the *dreidel* game to see how much *gelt* (gold-covered chocolate coins) they can win!

---

[45] Ibid., 73.

First night—light the *shammash*, the first candle.

> You won't need the sun to brighten the day or the moon and lamps to give you light. The Eternal One will be all the light you ever need. Your God will provide your glory, brilliance for all time. (Isaiah 60:19)

Second night—light the *shammash* and use it to light the second candle.

> Because, although you were once the personification of darkness, you are now light in the Lord. So act like children of the light. For the fruit of the light is all that is good, right and true. Make it your aim to learn what pleases the Lord. Don't get involved with the fruitless works of darkness: instead, expose them to the light of God. (Ephesians 5:8–11)

Third night—light the *shammash* and use it to light the second and third candles.

> But if someone responds to and obeys His word, then God's love has truly taken root and filled him. This is how we know we are in an intimate relationship with Him: anyone who says, "I live in intimacy with Him," should walk the path Jesus walked. My loved ones, in one sense, I am writing a new command for you. I am only reminding you of the old command. It's a word you already know, a word that has existed from the beginning. However, in another sense, I am writing a new command for you. The new command is the truth that he lived; and now you are

living it too because the darkness is fading and the true light is already shining among you. (1 John 1:5–9)

Fourth night—light the *shammash* and use it to light the second, third, and fourth candles.

> On another occasion, Jesus spoke to the crowds again. "I Am the light that shines through the cosmos; if you walk with Me, you will thrive in the nourishing light that gives life and will not know darkness." (John 8:12)

Fifth night—light the *shammash* and use it to light second, third, fourth, and fifth candles.

> It was winter and time for the Festival of Dedication.[a] While in Jerusalem, Jesus was walking through the temple in an area known as Solomon's porch, and Jews gathered around Him. (John 10:22–24)

Sixth night—light the *shammash* and use it to light second, third, fourth, fifth, and sixth candles.

> Your word is a lamp for my steps; it lights the path before me. When Your words are unveiled, light shines forth; they bring understanding to the simple. (Psalm 119:105, 130)

> For their direction is a lamp; their instruction will light your path, and their discipline will correct your missteps, sending you down the right path of life. (Proverbs 6:23)

Seventh night—light the *shammash* and use it to light the second to the seventh candles.

> The eye is the lamp of the body. You draw light into your body through your eyes, and light shines out to the world through your eyes. So if your eye is well and shows you what is true, then your whole body will be filled with light. (Matthew 6:22–23)

Eighth night—light the *shammash* and use it to light second to the eighth candles.

> Light is among you, but very soon it will flicker out. Walk as you have the light, and then the darkness will not surround you. Those who walk in darkness don't know where they are going. While the light is with you, believe in the light; and you will be reborn as sons and daughters of the light. (John 12:35–36)

See appendix 2 for the full *Hanukkah* liturgy and comments for each night.

Hanukkah food

Traditional *Hanukkah* foods are fried in oil! If you are health conscious and don't want to eat a lot of fried food, it is possible to bake most of the dishes and have a wonderful meal. Either way, there are many sites to find recipes and meal plans for this feast. At my house, we only do one big meal with as many people who can come! It is really almost impossible to do a big celebratory meal for eight nights! Although, I will say that it is possible to have wonderful leftovers if you make enough the first night!

The must-haves are fried apples or applesauce and latkes (potato pancakes).

See appendix 1 for recipes.

Advent

There are many similarities between Advent, *Hanukkah*, and Christmas. They all complement each other in ways that can help us see and experience the past, revel in the present, and hope for the future.

In our home, we have an Advent wreath with four candles that represent the four Sundays before Christmas. Most churches these days will also have an Advent wreath set up and will have various congregants that represent the various age groups in the church family light the candles each week with a special reading and prayer. At home, I light a candle each week and read a brief devotion that helps me reflect on the theme for the week. The next week, I light an additional candle and repeat until Christmas Day when I light all four candles and the Christ candle as my husband reads the Christmas story from Luke 2.

Advent is about anticipation. It leads us to Christmas. Children so look forward to Christmas and getting and giving presents. This journey of anticipation can help young children especially learn to focus and enjoy the anticipation of Christmas Day! Give your children the opportunity to light a candle, read a verse, and talk about the angels, the shepherds, and Mary and Joseph and recount parts of the story that they know.

The traditional colors for the Advent candles are three purple and one pink. I recall thinking, many years ago, *Why are the candles those awful colors, and how come they aren't all the same color?* I didn't know much at that time but have since learned about the colors and what they represent!

The traditional themes for each of the four weeks of Advent are hope, peace, joy, and love. The purple candles represent royalty. Jesus's heritage is from the line of King David. The third candle is the pink or rose candle representing joy. Sometimes, the third Sunday of Advent is referred to as *Gaudete* Sunday. *Gaudete* is a Latin word meaning "rejoice." In the midst of all the preparation and reflection on the deeper meaning of the season, there is this moment of joyfulness. It is a respite from the other Sundays that reflect on the earthly ministry of Jesus. On this Sunday, we rejoice with the angel who made the greatest proclamation of all time to a bunch of unsuspecting shepherds! "Listen! I bring good news, news of great joy, news that will affect all people everywhere..." (Luke 2:8).

During Advent, we see Jesus as an adult and work backward to his birth. The Sunday before Advent, we proclaim Christ as King. Christ is King over all, in all, and through all. So it helps us in the journey to Bethlehem to view his earthly life backward. "As a transition into Advent, the Sunday devoted to the reign of Christ enables us to grasp more fully the Advent promise of the One who shall be called 'the Prince of peace' and presses upon us the need to 'seek peace and pursue it(1 Peter 3:11).'"[46]

It is in this time of anticipation that we are to slow down our lives and our thinking. This is so contrary to what our culture tells us we should do. Culture says we should be rushing here and there to get our shopping done, our decorating done, our baking done, and then completely crashes after all the entertaining and festivities are over! And then make New Year's resolutions to get back in shape, spend less money, and refocus our mental and spiritual state!

My husband and I decided a number of years ago to not let culture dictate our lives. Even as our daughters were getting married and our son was growing up, we put great restraint on the spending and worked on focusing on the importance of God in our lives rather than on presents that ultimately wear out. As our grandchildren came along, we made careful choices about gifts and wanted to give them

---

[46] Laurence Hull Stookey, *Calendar: Christ's Time for the Church* (Nashville, TN: Abingdon Press, 1996), 140.

gifts that had long-term implications rather than short-term value. These days, we make a contribution to an organization that helps others and send each grandchild a card telling them what was given in their honor. We have also invited them to share in our celebrations of the biblical feasts as they are able. This is an important way that we can help them see themselves as part of the story of God.

The early church fathers developed a system for helping people in their faith journey to experience the mystery of their faith. St. Bernard of Clairvaux (1090–1153) was a theologian who contributed the church's theology of Advent. In one of his sermons, he laid out that Advent had a threefold order of time. He said this was evidenced in time past, time present, and time future.[47] During this time, we look for the coming of the Messiah in Bethlehem (Micah 5:2–4) and the coming Messiah at the end of time (Isaiah 65:17–25; Revelation 20–22)."[48]

Over time, church leaders developed themes that helped people in this season of expectation and hope. I find that having this kind of roadmap helps me stay focused on what is truly important. It was actually Pope Gregory I (590–604) who determined that a four-Sunday Advent season "with its strong eschatological orientation"[49] should be practiced, and this is where the four themes, one for each Sunday, have roots.

The first week of Advent, *hope* is the theme. This is both a look back as well as a look forward. The Jews hoped for a promised Messiah. In ancient times, every young Jewish girl knew that there would one day come a Messiah who would save the Jewish people. So it was that Mary was not unfamiliar with this idea when the angel of the Lord appeared to her to tell her of what was to come. Every Jewish mama wanted her daughter to bear the child that would be the Messiah!

---

[47] Martin Connell, *Eternity Today: On the Liturgical Year,* vol 1. (New York, NY: Continuum, 2006), 53.

[48] Robert E. Webber, *Ancient-Future Time: Forming Spirituality through the Christian Year* (Grand Rapids, MI: Baker Books, 2004), 44.

[49] Paul F. Bradshaw and Maxwell E. Johnson, *The Origins of Feasts, Fasts and Seasons in Early Christianity* (Collegeville, MN: SPCK, 2011), 158.

The prophet Isaiah foretold of a coming Messiah that would save the people. In Isaiah's day, the world was in turmoil, politically and spiritually. The worship in Israel had become stagnant and ritualistic. The people were a mess! Isaiah's words to the people were to give them renewed hope and infuse new life into their worship. He told them of One who would come to save them and restore the greatness of Jerusalem. He also told them of the One who would come to give his very life for their salvation. Salvation was from their personal sin in rejecting God and his commands. The One who saves would also be the One who would restore. And this would be not only for the Jews but for all the people of the world! Jesus would be the Child who would come to be the savior of sins and then complete his final work when he comes again as King of kings!

The theme for the second Sunday in Advent is *peace*. There are many verses of scripture that talk about peace, and by this time, we are ready for some peace after all the rush-rush-rush of preparations for Christmas! But this is really about being *at* peace in our hearts and minds, peace with one another, and the fulfillment of peace in eternity when Christ will come again. In Isaiah 9:6, the prophet gives him special names: Wonderful Counselor, Mighty God, Eternal Father, Prince of Peace. My favorite blessing is the Aaronic blessing found in Number 6:24–26, "The Eternal One bless you and keep you, May He make his face shine upon you and be gracious to you. The Eternal lift up His countenance to look upon you and give you peace."

Whether we only gather at home or we gather together with our church family, what a marvelous way to go into the week knowing that the very face of the Eternal One is looking over each one of us! This can be very comforting for all members of the family.

The third week of Advent, the theme is *joy.* The candle that is lit this Sunday is pink. I think this is my favorite Sunday of Advent! The music may be more upbeat as we are called to reflect on the joy that Mary must have known as she gave birth to the Holy Child (Luke 2:6, 19), the joy the shepherds felt as they heard the angels announcement (Luke 2:8–18), the magi experienced when they saw the star (Matthew 2:10), the joy when someone comes to faith in Christ and believes (Luke 15:10), the fruit of the Spirit that lives within each believer in Jesus Messiah! (Galatians 5:22), and the joy that comes when like-minded people gather together for fellowship (Philippians 2:2).

The fourth week of Advent, the theme is *love*. Christ came to demonstrate his love for us. Romans 5:8, "But think about this: while we were wasting our lives in sin, God revealed His powerful love to us in a tangible display—the Anointed One died for us." The ultimate gift of all gifts was Christ's death on the cross so that we could be saved!

May this Advent season be a very special time for you and your family, near or far, gathered together or separated. Remember that the church far and wide is also gathering, virtually or in person, to anticipate the coming of Messiah! We all eagerly await his coming!

See appendix 2 for an Advent liturgy at home.

Advent/Christmas decorations

We just *love* decorating for Christmas at my house! I do have a dream that one year, I will slowly decorate each week with the culmination of the tree being fully decorated on Christmas Eve! I think this is really a pipe dream! But, this past year, I almost accomplished it! When *Hanukkah* lands in early December, I can major on decorating for *Hanukkah* first. I dedicate a whole room to just *Hanukkah* decorations. When *Hanukkah* is over, out come the rest of the Christmas decorations. I do have to really think through ahead of time how to make this all work, but from past years, I know I will be satisfied with how it all turns out.

In the past couple of decades, I have become more and more intentional about what ornaments go on my main Christmas tree. I say "main" because I have trees in almost every room of my house! So the main tree is what I lovingly call the "Wonderful Counselor, Mighty God, Prince of Peace" tree. The ornaments that get put on this tree reflect the names of Jesus and the themes of Advent:

hope, peace, joy, and love. I use Chrismon symbols also on this tree. Chrismons are symbols of the Christian faith.

Years ago, I found a needlepoint pattern for making Chrismons, and there was a person in our church who did beautiful needlepoint. (I served as worship leader of a small church in northern California at the time and began to teach the church about the seasons of the church year). I asked the woman if she would make the Chrismons, following the pattern I had found, and she did! They were works of art, and people responded well to her serving the church with her gift!

Many years later, I met a woman in Calgary, at a craft fair, who tatted (not tattoos)! Tatting is an art form of lace making. I asked her if she knew what Chrismons were and she did not. So we had quite a conversation, and she got really excited about creating something new! She now comes up with a new design each year. Her intricate creations now adorn my tree. I have even hung some of them on ribbon and placed them on a wall so that they are more prominently displayed.

My color scheme for Christmas has changed somewhat over the years, but this past year, I think I finally found the design I have been trying to achieve. My main color scheme has evolved into white, silver, gold, and glass. Yours might be different, and you should do what gives you joy and pleases your family! If you make ornaments or your children make ornaments, display them prominently! Everyone most likely has a favorite ornament and perhaps a story to go along with it! Play Christmas music as you decorate, and sing at the top of your voices!

In my previous home I had a mantle over my fireplace, and last year, I found white stockings trimmed with gold. I used all white candles with a bit of greenery on the mantel. This is also where I put the magi and a camel. My Nativity scene was on another low table in the same room. Eventually, I would move the magi and camel into the Nativity scene, take out the shepherds, and replace baby Jesus with Mary and an older child. Remember, the magi came later, perhaps as much as two years later.

A fun idea for children to work on during Advent is a Jesse tree. A Jesse tree can be made of real, or fake, bare branches. It is a family tree that traces the roots or historical lineage of Jesus beginning with Jesse, the father of King David. Isaiah 11:1–4 is the backdrop for the symbol of the Jesse tree. [50] This would be a great time to tell family stories of your own heritage so that young children especially learn to relate their history with the lineage of Jesus.

"But on this humbled ground, a tiny shoot, Hopeful and promising, will sprout from Jesse's stump; A branch will emerge from his roots to bear fruit. And on this child from David's line, the Spirit of the Eternal One will alight and rest…"

Ornaments that have names or pictures of the bible characters can be hung on the tree. Children can create artwork that symbolizes the characters and events leading up to the birth of Jesus. This is a great activity for Sunday school students but can easily be adapted for home. It is much like an Advent calendar. Ornaments could be hung on the tree every day leading up to Christmas Day.

Advent calendars are another great way to help children and young ones eagerly wait for Christmas Day and help to tell the story of Jesus's birth. Advent calendars come in all kinds of presentations, but I like ones that tell a little bit of the true Christmas story every day. Perhaps you have a grandma who can make a reusable one for your children!

Christmas Eve and Christmas Day

Christmas Eve menu ideas

If I am not participating in Christmas Eve services at church, it is much easier to plan a lovely meal. I think soups are great on this night along with some special sweet treats! Other years, we have done appetizers and desserts. Who needs a big meal when there are lots of special treats to gobble up! If you are having family and friends in,

---

[50] https://www.whychristmas.com/customs/jessetrees.shtml

ask them to bring a favorite treat to share. Be sure to include telling stories about favorite memories into your celebration.

Most churches will have a Christmas Eve service where candles are lit, lots of carols are sung, and a special time is enjoyed in the celebration of communion (or Eucharist, depending on your church). The service may be held close to midnight or earlier for young families. The Christmas Eve service has typically been my favorite service of the year! I love the candles, the music, and the very specialness of it all! The church family gathers together one more time in great anticipation of the coming of Christ and reminds the world why he came as well as the promise that he will come again.

Due to COVID this past year, things have changed dramatically, and we found ourselves scaling way back on our celebrations. But where there is a will, there is a way! This is where technology is the next best thing! We Zoomed with some of our children, lit the Advent wreath, and read the Christmas story from Luke 2 together. Not too bad!

Christmas Day is the ultimate day of celebration! It is the culmination of the Advent Season and the beginning of the Christmas season! Notice I said "season" and not "day" as Christmas is not about just one day. But what a day for the celebration to begin! I love to make a special breakfast or brunch depending on who is already in the house or whom we are expecting. Typically, my husband will read the story from Luke 2 about the birth of Jesus and then from Matthew 2 about the magi and the gifts they brought to the Messiah. We open our stockings and any gifts to exchange. Then we eat! At this point in life, it is not so much about receiving gifts as it is about what we eat! I will say, though, that we have had some years when there were some very fun surprises in our stockings!

About every seven years, Christmas Day lands on a Sunday. I know many people who would rather skip church and just spend the day at home. I beg to differ. Christmas Day on a Sunday has even more significance as the church around the world gathers, at different times of the day, to worship the King of kings and Lord of lords! To sing "Joy to the World, the Lord *is* come" on Christmas Day with the gathered church is an amazing worship experience! To hear the story preached again sends it even deeper into my heart. I am humbled by knowing that the church universal is also hearing the Word and singing with the angels, "Glory to God in the highest, peace on earth…"

Christmas Day menu ideas

I love cheese blintzes on Christmas Day! They can be made ahead and even frozen so that it's not too much trouble to get them ready that morning. And it's not so much of a mess if they are prepared ahead of time! A winter fruit salad goes nicely along with a sweet bread and cranberry juice!

I love to set a nice table even if it's just the two of us. I use my crystal and silver place settings and pretty Christmas dishes. I even have some ruby-red lunch plates that are depression-era. My husband says I love to play house, and he is right!

Last summer, we moved to a retirement community where my aunt and uncle also live. They are just down the street from us, and now we are able to share the planning, decorating, and feasting together! We have even done one feast as a progressive dinner! Both of our husbands are good sports about all our ideas and the craziness that often ensues.

Christmas Day ushers in the period of the "Twelve Days of Christmas" or Christmastide. It's not about a song! Although, a case has been made about the "real" meaning behind the "Twelve Days of Christmas" song. Historically, it has not been proved that it was used as a secret code, but a tradition has come down that says that the twelve days represent a mnemonic device that helped children learn about the teachings of the early church. It is a fun way to think about it! If you want to know, here it is:

1. Partridge in a pear tree = represents Christ.
2. Turtle doves = both testaments.

3. French hens = faith, hope, and love, the theological virtues (1 Corinthians 13:13).

4. Calling (colly) birds = the four Gospels (Matthew, Mark, Luke, John).

5. Golden rings = the five books of Moses, the Pentateuch (Genesis, Exodus, Leviticus, Numbers, Deuteronomy).

6. Geese a-laying = the six days of creation (Genesis 1–2).

7. Swans a-swimming = the seven gifts of the Holy Spirit, the seven sacraments. There are more gifts of the Spirit listed in scripture in several different passages (i.e., 1 Corinthians 12–14; Ephesians 4). The seven sacraments practiced by the Catholic church are baptism, Eucharist (communion), confirmation, reconciliation, anointing of the sick, marriage, holy orders. Protestant churches today practice baptism and Eucharist (communion, Lord's Table) as the most significant sacraments in worship.

8. Maids a-milking = the eight beatitudes (Matthew 5).

9. Ladies dancing = the nine Fruit of the Spirit (Galatians 5:22).

10. 1 Lord a-leaping = the Ten Commandments (Deuteronomy 5).

11. Pipers piping = the eleven faithful apostles (Matthew 10).

12. Drummers drumming = the twelve points of doctrine in the Apostle's Creed.

I believe in God, the Father Almighty, maker of
    heaven and earth;
And in Jesus Christ, his only Son, our Lord; who
    was conceived by the
Holy Spirit, born of the virgin, Mary,
suffered under Pontius Pilate, was crucified,
    dead, and buried.
He descended into hell.
The third day he rose again from the dead.
He ascended into heaven, and sits on the right
    hand of God the Father
Almighty. From there he shall come to judge the
    quick and the dead.
I believe in the Holy Ghost, the holy catholic
    church, the communion of
saints, the forgiveness of sins, the resurrection of
    the body, and the life
everlasting. *Amen.*

Whew! It has been a whirlwind of a season! I don't know about
you, but by this time of year, I am ready for a break! Guess what? The
next season of the church year includes what is known as Ordinary
Time. I am so ready for some Ordinary Time—time to put all the
decorations away and clean house.

Hannukah Décor includes menorah, gelt, dreidels

Hanukkah centerpiece

CHAPTER 5

Epiphany and Ordinary Time (Part 1)

Be still. Be patient. Expect the Eternal to arrive and set things right.
Don't get upset when you see the worldly ones rising up the ladder.
Don't be bothered by those who are anchored in wicked ways.

—*Psalm 37:7*

Civic Calendar: Martin Luther King Day—January
President's Birthdays: February
Church Calendar: Epiphany—January, Ash Wednesday: February

Christmastide concludes with Epiphany on January 6. The origin of Epiphany can be traced back to the third century. In the east, the day celebrated the baptism of Jesus. In the west, it was not until about the fourth century that the Magi were celebrated.[51] In my home, this is when I will move the Magi pieces into the Nativity scene. Previously, they have been somewhere else in the house!

Epiphany means "manifestation of Christ." Webster's dictionary defines it as "an appearance or manifestation especially of a divine being." January 6 was observed as a church festival commemorating the arrival of the Magi as described in Matthew 2. This feast day, in most evangelical churches, doesn't seem to get much attention. But

---

[51] Martin Connell, *Eternity Today: On the Liturgical Year*, vol. I (New York: Continuum International Publishing Group, 2006), 151, 163.

this short season can have a wonderful impact on our spiritual journey if we don't overlook it. Through Epiphany and Ordinary Time that follows, we can experience the manifestation of Christ in our own lives.

There are three events that are generally connected during the season of Ordinary Time: (1) the coming of the Magi, (2) the baptism of Jesus, and (3) the wedding feast at Cana. How can each of these events impact our lives? We can reflect on these events at home even if our church does not follow the practice of the church year. Certainly, the fact that the Magi were from different countries tells us that Christ came for the world, not only for the Jews.

The disciples were told to "go out into the world and share the good news with all of creation. Anyone who believes this good news and is ceremonially washed will be rescued..." (Mark 16:15–16). This is the greatest news of all! Jesus came not only to the Jew but also for the entire world! This includes you! Let that sink deeply into your being. Praise God for his good, good gift of salvation.

Reflecting on Jesus's baptism allows us to reflect on our own baptism and takes us deeper into the mystery of our faith. God brought the Israelites through the Red Sea and then crossed over the Jordan River into the promised land. The symbolism here is in passing from one way of life to another.

My father baptized me at the tender age of six. In order for me to be baptized, I had to be able to tell what it meant and why I wanted to do it. In my six-year-old level of understanding, I did know that Jesus died on the cross for me and that I needed and wanted to follow him. As I grew up, my understanding of the significance of this act of public declaration of my desire to be a follower of Christ came to bear.

Jesus was baptized by his cousin John in the Jordan River. Jesus was baptized for the sins of the people for whom he was going to die. John called Jesus the "Lamb who takes away the sin of the world!" (John 1:29). Jesus became the Lamb that would take away all our sins. There would be no more need for sacrifices.

Jesus's miracle at the wedding feast in Cana is significant because he did something that allowed others to shine. Remember the story? It's found in John chapter 2. Jesus and his disciples went to a wedding feast. In that culture, the wedding feast lasted for many days. Can you imagine? The family of the bride put on a huge party! But they had miscalculated how many people would come and how much food and drink to provide. So they ran out of wine.

Jesus's mother, Mary, went to Jesus and told him that it would be very embarrassing if the hosts ran out of wine. Jesus told the servers to fill up the large pots with water. They did as instructed. When they took a cup to the host, for tasting, the host was surprised that the wine was the best! In that culture, it was customary, and everyone knew this, that the best wine was served first and then as everyone was feeling good, the wine would be watered down. But this was not the case!

The significance of the miracle is that God has something better in store for those who wait on him. Follow his lead, do his will, and he will provide!

Thinking about these things and living them out in our daily lives commends us to be more and more aware of not only the earthly life of Christ but also the eternal impact.

Ordinary Time lasts until the Sunday before Ash Wednesday, about seven to eight weeks. Ordinary Time is also a short respite from the previously very busy season! Isn't it good to have downtime? That's what Ordinary Time is like—a time to rest and regroup, a time to reflect and give thanks and prepare for God to work.

"Day by day...Three things I pray: To see Thee more clearly, Love Thee more dearly, follow Thee more nearly..."[52]

---

[52] Lyrics by BMG Rights Management, Sony/ATV Music Publishing LLC, Spirit Music Group, Downtown Music Publishing, Warner Chappell Music, Inc.

CHAPTER 6

Ash Wednesday, Lent, Purim

His leadership will bring such prosperity as you've never seen before—sustainable peace for all time. This child: God's promise to David—a throne forever, among us, to restore sound leadership that cannot be perverted or shaken. He will ensure justice without fail and absolute equity. Always. The intense passion of the Eternal, Commander of heavenly armies, will carry this to completion.
—Isaiah 9:7

Christian Calendar: Ash Wednesday, Lent—February, March–April
    (40 days)
Biblical Calendar: Purim—March

Ash Wednesday is being recovered in many Protestant churches today. The significance of the ashes and the cross are historical. "In the early days of the church, new Christians were signed with the cross and told that the cross was an invisible tattoo (many people in the Roman era wore tattoos symbolizing their vocation)."[53] Ashes are another powerful biblical symbol that signifies repentance. Both of these symbols mark the beginning of Lent and help us focus on the importance of our own spiritual condition. An Ash Wednesday

---

[53] Robert E. Webber, *Rediscovering the Christian Feasts: A Study in the Services of the Christian Year* (Peabody, MA: Hendrickson, 1998), 42, 43.

service focuses our attention on our spiritual condition. There may or may not be any music. Prayers that are offered lead the worshipper to a place of acknowledging sin and asking for forgiveness. Scripture that is read reflects on our personal need for spiritual renewal. In Matthew 6, Jesus calls us to practice prayer, almsgiving, and fasting. This is a season to put into practice the things we believe. These practices are not perfunctory but help us live in relationship with God and in community with each other.[54]

An interesting practice in some churches has been the burning of palm branches from Palm Sunday. The palms would be left to dry and then burned. The ashes that result would be saved and used on the next Ash Wednesday. Doing this connects the two events together and reminds the worshipper that all have sinned, need to repent, and accept forgiveness (Romans 8:28).

Lent

Lent begins on Ash Wednesday and is counted for forty days, not counting Sundays, until Easter. Sundays are not included because each Sunday is set aside for corporate worship and praise. The forty days of Lent has early church origins, but it wasn't until about the fourth century that the practice was solidified into the forty days of prayer, fasting, and almsgiving.

Traditionally, during this period of forty days before Easter, people will decide to do something to help them remember why this season is important. Historically, Lenten practices have been fasting, praying, and almsgiving. Lenten practices might be "giving up" something for Lent like not eating any candy or sugar. This is only effective if it is done in conjunction with intentional prayer, meditation, and scripture reading. If you truly desire to deepen your relationship with God, then it might be more effective to "do" something.

Spiritual disciplines are good, and there are so many ways to be creative and build a new discipline that strengthens your relationship

---

[54] *Ancient-Future Time: Forming Spirituality through the Christian Year* (Grand Rapids, MI: BakerBooks, 2004) 101, 102.

with God, blesses others, and benefits you! You may know people who say they are giving up something like coffee or chocolate for Lent. Why do they do that? Have you ever had the nerve to ask? The answer might be that it's tradition. Or they think that it's a good thing for them to do. But that kind of rationale is not sufficient. Building spiritual discipline is a good reason and should at least be accompanied by prayer and scripture reading so that one's relationship with God is growing deeper.

If you have young children, perhaps your family could come up with ideas to foster spiritual discipline. Some ideas might be for everyone in the family to memorize a portion of scripture together. At the end of the forty days, how many verses will you have committed to memory? Psalm 119:11 says, "Deep within me I have hidden Your word so that I will never sin against You."

Another idea for a family might be to take turns doing something nice for another member of the family in secret. Have a reveal party on Easter! Or don't reveal and let the mystery continue!

One of my practices has been to email notes of encouragement to each of my students. I would figure out how many students to send emails to each day so that every student got a personal word of encouragement from me. I did not send out a mass email but a personal word for each one. This way, I could also pray that the Lord would give me the right words to say to as I typed special words of encouragement. Students appreciated the personable message of the emails, and sometimes I would get a note back telling me that my words had come at just the right time!

I have also sent text messages to my adult children every day during Lent with verses of encouragement. Whatever you decide, let it be meaningful, and the practice will become a good habit as well as a blessing to you and others. This is a special time set aside to think more deeply about our own spiritual journey and assess where we are in our relationship with God. I find that doing even small things help me remember why I am doing it and what it means to me. It also allows me moments to reflect on the goodness of God, his grace, provision, and blessing. As I reach out to others, it allows me moments to praise God for each one, pray over them, and be thankful for them.

Purim

Purim is the most joyful and crazy celebration! It is a costume party with a story of good versus evil, a beautiful princess, and a horrible, evil man. It almost sounds like a Disney movie! But it's even better than Disney because it really happened! The story of Esther is a story of faith and triumph over tragedy. The festival of *Purim* is not listed in the feasts and festival in Leviticus 23 because it did not happen until much later. The events of the story began about 2500 years ago in the land of Persia (now Iran). The Jews had been taken captive years before from the land of Israel to Babylon. They began to make a life there but tried to maintain their traditional way of life as the chosen of God. They had assimilated to a certain degree but, most likely, lived in communities that were distant from the Persians.

The king held a huge banquet and had invited all the princes and officials from all the provinces to come to the capital. The banquet lasted for 180 days! Can you even begin to imagine? There were parades, parties, banquets, and all types of festivities. Then there was another special week of festivals for all who lived in the capital. It was during this week that the story really gets exciting! The king sent for the queen to come and dance before all the invited guests. The queen refused. As a result, she was banished. Haman, one of the king's closest advisers, urged the king to hold a beauty contest. Mordecai, a Jew who worked in the palace, told his niece, Esther, that she should participate but not to tell anyone that she was a Jew. Esther won the contest, and the king was totally smitten with her. Other palace intrigue ensued, and a plot was discovered by Mordecai that some very bad people wanted to kill the king. The plot was adverted and recorded in the annals of the king.

One night, the king had trouble sleeping, so he called for his scribe to come and read something boring, like the chronicles, so that he could get back to sleep. It was during this reading that the story of the plot to kill the king came to light. The king wanted to know what had been done to honor the person who discovered the plot. "Nothing," said the scribe.

The king called Haman and asked what should be done to honor someone that the king wants to show favor. Haman thought it was him! It wasn't! It was Mordecai, Haman's nemesis.

Haman was so angry that he and his henchmen devised a plot to not only get rid of Mordecai but all the Jews throughout the land. He did this by telling the king that there were people who refused to bow down to him. The king bought in and signed a decree that could not be revoked. On a certain day, all the Jews were to be destroyed.

Mordecai discovered this and sent word to Esther insisting that she tell the king. Esther held a couple of banquets for the king and Haman and got up the nerve to tell the king of Haman's plot. She also told the king that the people Haman wanted to destroy would include her.

The king was furious but knew he could not revoke his own decree. An alternative would need to be arranged so that the Jews could defend themselves against anyone who tried to kill them. At the end, Mordecai sent out a decree to all the land that the Jews were to celebrate their deliverance with food and drink, to send gifts, and to offer help to the poor (Esther 9:20–22). The celebration was to be commemorated every year.

The name *Purim* means "lots." Casting "lots" was a game of chance, much like throwing dice, used to make decisions. This is where the name originated. Did you read the book of Esther? Chapter 3 is where you will find the description.

Here is some backstory: the Israelites went through many trials and tribulations as their story has unfolded through time. When they disobeyed the Lord's commands, they suffered consequences. Disease, famine, and all sorts of bad things happened to them. They were often conquered by surrounding countries and taken off to distant lands by their captors. But God was always faithful in his promise to return them to the land of their forefathers: Abraham, Isaac, and Jacob. As the story of Esther begins, the Israelites (referred to as Jews for the first time) have been in Persia for a while. Some had been allowed to return to Jerusalem (see the story in Nehemiah). Those who remained were trying to maintain a way of life passed down from previous generations. God has always provided a way for his people to return to Him. This story is a story of faith, persecution against incredible odds, and victory.

So after you have read the entire ten chapters of the book of Esther, you can see how God definitely had a hand in delivering his chosen people even though his name is not mentioned in the book! In chapter 9, Mordecai was constantly in touch with the Jewish community and reminding them to remember and celebrate the days when "their sadness turned into gladness and their mourning into celebration. He encouraged them to celebrate with food and drink, to send gifts, and to offer help to the poor" (verses 22–23). So now it is time to *party*!

We have been organizing and planning *Purim* parties for the last couple of years now. We have done it differently each time depending on who is coming and the age range of participants. Orthodox Jews will read from the *megillah* (a scroll) the night before the celebration and again on the day of celebration. It is also tradition to dress up in fun costumes! This represents God's hand in the *Purim* miracle which was disguised by natural events.[55] Then the day climaxes with a great meal and taking gifts of food to others and giving to those in need.

For our parties at home, here is how we have celebrated:

The first time we hosted a *Purim* party, we decided that we would read the book of Esther in dramatic style. *The Voice* Bible was our resource for the script. We assigned parts, and before our meal, we read the story out loud. It took quite a while to do this! The next year, I rewrote the narrative as a play, shortening it a lot, mostly for the sake of time but also because we had young ones participate in the drama. I emailed the scripts, with character assignments, out ahead of time so that the grandkids could rehearse with mom

---

[55] https://www.chabad.org/holidays/purim/article_cdo/aid/1362/jewish/Purim-How-To-Guide.htm#Masquerade (Accessed 3/25/2020).

and dad and become familiar with the characters and their speaking parts. My aunt, Martha Amster Hodges, provided home-constructed masks and props for each of the participants in our play. That year, it happened to be a lovely warm day, so we held our play outside on the patio. We set up chairs for those not "on stage" to sit and be the audience. We designated an area for the play, and everyone followed the script. This was really fun! The grandkids did an awesome job of reading their lines and acting out their characters. We also supplied everyone not on stage with noisemakers so that whenever Haman was speaking or mentioned, he would be drowned out by the noise!

This past year, our grandkids were not able to come, so we got even more creative with only four participants. We made a game out of the storytelling. I moved furniture around in my living room (it was too chilly to do outside this year!) and put all of the masks and props on a low square table. The script, this time, consisted of the names of all the characters in the story with bullet points to help us remember the events and the sequence. Everyone chose a mask to wear.

Basically, the rules for the game are as follows:

1. Decide who will go first. Person 1 puts on a costume and begins the story. When person 1 stops, another person quickly puts on another costume and continues.
2. While person 2 is telling the story, others can put costumes on and be ready to jump in with the next part of the story.
3. Repeat until the story has been told to everyone's satisfaction!

We had a lot of fun doing this, and certainly, part of that fun was getting the props and costumes on! This works well when there are only a few people as each person can play more than one role. That also makes for lots of laughter! Be sure to have lots of noisemakers on hand and blow them whenever Haman speaks or is mentioned.

We had decided to eat first and then do our play-game and then have dessert. We felt we had worked up quite an appetite after all that prop and costume changing! Of course, we also took some pictures so we have fun memories!

Remember at the beginning of this book, I said that we live under grace, not only by the law. So with that in mind, I think it is very fair to be creative; come up with your own way of remembering and telling the story. Remember also that God works in very mysterious ways even today. Seeing how he is constantly involved in history helps us to see how he is also involved in our lives today.

Esther is a great story of deliverance. Even though God is not specifically mentioned in the story, it is very clear that he orchestrated all of the events to bring about his promise to deliver his people. As you may recall, God delivered his people so many times from very difficult circumstances!

As I mentioned, we had dinner first. You may decide that doing your play works better before your meal. It really is up to you! We recited the blessings and prayed before the meal. There are three traditional blessings:

1. Blessed are You, O Lord our God, King of the universe, who has sanctified us with His commandments and commanded us concerting the reading of the megillah (the story of Esther). Amen.
2. Blessed are You, O Lord our God, King of the universe, who performed miracles for our forefathers in those days at this time. Amen.
3. Blessed are You, O Lord our God, King of the universe, who has granted us life and enabled us to reach this occasion. Amen.

See appendix 2 for both versions of the story of *Purim*.

Do you see the connection between this event and the Lenten season? Both point us to God's saving grace and draw us into knowing him better. I hope that you are beginning to see and understand how the appointed seasons and festivals that God commanded his people in ancient times and the seasons of the church year come together so that we are constantly being drawn closer into fellowship with Jesus. As you read and tell the story, it becomes even clearer that God's fingerprints are all through the story! His fingerprints should be all through our story as well!

Decoration ideas

I purchased several masks, brightly colored bead necklaces, and ribbons from my favorite dollar store. I glued masks onto wooden skewers that I had wrapped with the ribbons and made an arrangement of them in a vase and placed on my table. I used some colored votives, more masks, and beads arranged on a table runner. I had purchased some toy *groggers* while in Israel last year and arranged them on the table as well. A *grogger* is a ratchet-like toy with a handle that makes a rattling noise when you spin it. They are made out of wood or plastic. I also had some New Year's Eve noisemakers left from last year and placed them among the masks and *groggers*. The groggers and noisemakers are to be used whenever Haman's name is mentioned. Booing and hissing are also recommended, much like at a melodrama when the villain is speaking!

Costume ideas

Costumes can be as simple or elaborate as you want! The ideas can come from the story as well as your own imagination! We used masks purchased from the local dollar store, plastic necklaces, decorated hats made from oatmeal cartons, props cut out from cardboard and covered with aluminum foil.

Menu ideas

I must tell you about dessert first. *Hamantaschen* is a must! These tricornered cookies are fun to make and can be filled with all sorts of yumminess! You can fill them with any kind of jam, lemon curd, chocolate chips, or halvah (a crushed sesame seed treat that comes in vanilla, chocolate, or marble). I like to make a variety of them! For the main meal, we have done kabobs with lamb or beef. We also like a Mediterranean quinoa salad, zucchini with red bell pepper salad, couscous with peas, or other spring vegetables.

Purim meal: Falafels, Mediterranean salad

Purim décor with noise makers and groggers

Purim masks

CHAPTER 7

Holy Week, Passover, Feast of Unleavened Bread, Easter

For God expressed His love for the world in this way: He gave His only Son so that whoever believes in Him will not face everlasting destruction, but will have everlasting life.

—John 3:16

Church Calendar: Holy Week—March/April
Biblical Calendar: Passover, Feast of Unleavened Bread—April

Holy Week begins with Palm/Passion Sunday. Lent is coming to a close this week as we begin to really focus on Jesus our Messiah and what he came to do for us. Palm Sunday is a festive day and is often ushered in by the waving of palm branches, children singing, and the congregation lifting their voices together singing or shouting, "Hosanna! Blessed is he who comes in the name of the Lord!" The story of the triumphal entry of Jesus into Jerusalem is told with exuberance! But the day ends on a minor chord as it points to the end of the week and the passion of our Lord Jesus Christ. This week is the most sacred of all in the church calendar.

Passover may also begin during this week. Depending on the calendar, it may fall in the next week. I like it best when it falls during Holy Week as it helps tell the story of Jesus's mission to redeem all people from their sin. Remember that God's story began in Genesis. The redemption that God planned from the beginning of earthly history began with creation and Adam and Eve. Adam and Eve sinned, and so God made a plan for their redemption just as there is a way for us to be redeemed. Through the story of God's chosen people, he unfolded how redemption would take place. Through sign and symbol, God gave indications of how redemption for all of humanity would be achieved. God would send his only Son to be the ultimate sacrifice for sin, and all who believe in him would be saved eternally (John 3:16).

Passover began back in the time after the Israelites had been in Egypt for four hundred years. The reason the Israelites were in Egypt was because there had been a famine in Canaan, and Jacob's sons traveled to Egypt to buy grain. Many years before this, Jacob's sons had sold their younger brother, Joseph, to be a slave to a band of merchants who were heading to Egypt. Read this story in Genesis 37–50.

The book of Exodus begins by telling the story of how the Israelites populated an area called Goshen. They became so numerous that they were forced into slavery by the Egyptian Pharaoh because he didn't want them to become so powerful and numerous and make war against him. The rest of this story is what Passover is all about. But it is also very much part of God's story and how he revealed himself to his chosen people and promised to deliver them from slavery and lead them to the land that he had promised to Abraham.

"Passover" is a reference to the last plague where the Angel of Death "passed over" the houses that had the blood of a lamb painted on the doorposts and lintel of the doors. The people had been told to roast the lamb and eat it with bitter herbs and unleavened bread. They were to stay indoors but be ready to travel. The Angel of Death would kill the firstborn of every household that did not have blood on the doorposts. Death came to all of the households in Egypt, including Pharaoh's palace.

When Pharaoh finally told Moses to take all the Israelites and get out of Egypt, they were ready to go! Everything was packed up, and as they left, they went to their Egyptian neighbors and asked them for gold, jewels, and clothing (Exodus 12).

Later, after the Israelites had crossed the Red Sea, the Lord commanded the Israelites to commemorate this event with a special feast. They were to celebrate it every year in order to remember how the Lord had delivered them from the Egyptians. During Holy Week, we remember what the Lord has done for us. Just as the Lord commanded the Israelites to kill a lamb and sprinkle its blood, so the Son of God came to shed his blood. Later, when the Israelites were camping in the desert, God gave Moses directions to build a tabernacle where animals were sacrificed for the sins of the people. Jesus Christ became the final sacrifice for all time.

God's story is woven throughout history. It is his way of demonstrating to the world that his design for all humanity is to live in relationship with him.

At the Passover *Seder*, the telling of the Exodus story is primary. Foods are used to help tell the story. A *Haggadah*, the telling, is read with everyone at the table participating in telling the story, singing songs, reading scripture, eating, and drinking the special foods that represent the various parts of the story. The food symbols are placed on a special platter called a *Seder* plate. This special plate has seven indentations that hold each of the special food items. The elements that are placed on the plate are bitter herbs, parsley, horseradish, chopped apples and nuts, a lamb shank bone, a roasted egg, and, in the center, a small bowl of salted water. On the table, at each place setting is a cup of wine or grape juice. Another plate of *matzo* is also on the table as are candles. Each of these items is very significant, but three are essential. The *matzo* is a form of unleavened bread. It is made without yeast. It symbolized the haste of the Israelites in preparation for departing Egypt. Jesus said, "I am the bread of life. He who comes to me shall not hunger, and he who believes in me shall never thirst" (John 6:35). Jesus, our Messiah, is clearly seen symbolically in the unleavened bread.

This is also the Feast of Unleavened Bread. Three pieces of *matzo* are important for this and stacked on top of each other. The middle one is broken in half and one of the halves is wrapped in a napkin and hidden or "buried." An *afikomen* cover is used for this part of the celebration. An *afikomen* cover has three sections inside it. A single *matzo* is placed in each section. The middle is the one broken, half put back inside, and the other half wrapped and hidden somewhere. This can become a game for any children present to play "hide-and-seek" to find the hidden *matzo* and have it "redeemed." Redeeming the *matzo* means that the one who finds it gets some kind of a prize from the papa. It is this piece of *matzo* that is the last to be eaten at the end of the meal and savored as a reminder of things to come. The redeemed *matzo* is also a symbol of Jesus's resurrection and return—his second coming! As we eat the final piece, we shout together, "Next year, in Jerusalem!" Literally, it is fun to think about celebrating Passover in Israel. But how much more exciting to think of it in the New Jerusalem when Jesus returns to earth to reign as King of kings and Lord of lords!

Do you see any connections in the three pieces of *matzo*? The three represent several things: the Trinity, the Hebrew fathers Abraham, Isaac, and Jacob, and the three days that Jesus was in the tomb. The broken *matzo* represents Jesus's broken body on the cross. He was then buried and rose from the dead three days later.

The shank bone is also essential as it represents the sacrifice of an unblemished lamb. Since it can be difficult to get a shank bone from a local butcher, I have created a paper representation of one and put that on my *Seder* plate. The bone represents also the purity of the lamb/Lamb who took our place and died for our sins. Jesus was the fulfillment of the lamb that was killed in Egypt and whose blood was painted on the doorposts and lintel. Without the lamb, there could not be a Passover or deliverance. Without Jesus's shed blood, there is no forgiveness of sin (Matthew 26:28). He was sacrificed for all, Jew and Gentile alike! The *Seder* meal then is also a memorial of the Israelites being delivered and as well as all of humanity being saved by believing in the shed blood of the ultimate sacrifice made by Jesus Christ! Those who believe in Jesus, the Messiah, come to the table with thankfulness and humbleness for being saved from sin.

The bitter herbs (*maror*) represent the four hundred years that the Israelites were in Egypt and the slavery that they were forced into by Pharaoh (Exodus 1). The horseradish (*maror*) is eaten with *matzo* in order to remind us of the cruelty and harshness of being enslaved. The bitterness reminds us of our own sin and things that enslave us today.

The other items on the *Seder* plate—the parsley (*karpas*), salted water, roasted egg, and apples and nut mixture (*haroset*)—are also significant. The parsley is dipped into the salted water to represent the tears that were shed while in captivity. The roasted egg represents spring and new life. The apple-nut mixture represents the bricks that the Israelites were forced to make for the Egyptians.

Planning a *Seder* meal takes quite a bit of preparation. We start planning it several weeks in advance. Since Passover usually coincides with Holy Week, it takes lots of thought and preparation to execute all the elements in an orderly fashion. The first thing is deciding on the menu. Our basic menu stays the same, but recipes vary from year to year. We really like brisket, so I start looking for one at the grocer's a couple of weeks, if not a month, ahead of time. I also start making a guest list and inviting family and friends for the celebration.

The *Seder* plate is the central figure of the day, so that makes up my centerpiece. I also place candles on the table for warmth and atmosphere. Because we usually have many people around our table, I construct mini *Seder* plates for each person at each place setting as it is too difficult for everyone to reach the large *Seder* plate in the center of the table!

Now is definitely the time to use the very best dishes and serving pieces and pull the table out as far as it will go!

Decoration ideas

Besides the *Seder* plate in the center of the table, create mini *Seder* plates for each person at the table. It is much easier than passing the large plate around, especially if you have many guests. If you have several children, look for ways to help them enjoy the proceedings and have some fun! For instance, one year, I found small candies to represent each of the ten plagues. I put a few candies in a small muffin cup and placed ten cups at each child's plate. My aunt Martha made very cute illustrated pictures for each plague along with ones that said, "Let my people go!" During the part of the story when Moses is trying to get Pharaoh to let the people depart, the children raised their symbols and shouted, "Let my people go!" When each of the plagues was named, the children held up the symbol and then ate the candy. Adults may want to do this too because it is really fun!

I set my table with my grandmother's china, use the good silver and stemware. I add two stems for each person, one filled with wine (or grape juice) and one for water. I made some napkin rings with one-and-a-half-inch wide burlap and lace and glued a plastic frog on each one. I have a very long white tablecloth and matching napkins that I use for this special day. I also use gold charger plates so to avoid any drips from the wine glasses!

Also, on a small side table, I place a decorative hand towel and my cup of purification filled with water. This is a very special cup that has two handles. During the reading of the *Haggadah*, people are to ceremonially wash their hands. In order to be "clean," you cannot touch what is not "clean." So hold the cup in one hand and pour water over the other hand. The watered hand is now "clean." Take the other handle and pour water over the first hand. The first hand is now "clean."

Somewhere on your table, make a small place for the cup of Elijah. This doesn't have to be a full-place setting, just a special cup for Elijah in case he comes! Remember that Elijah is a picture of Christ whom we do expect to return at any moment!

You will need something to use as the *afikomen* cover. An *afikomen* cover is a beautifully decorated napkin with three pockets. If you don't have one, you can use three large napkins, unfolded, and laid on top of each other. When it is time to break the middle *matzo*, wrap half of the broken one in the middle napkin and "bury" it between the other two napkins. Wrap the other broken half of the *matzo* in another napkin. Have all the children cover their eyes while this matzo is hidden somewhere in the house.

Each person should have their own *Haggadah.* You can preassign reading parts for your guests. There are many parts that are read in unison, questions to be read by a child, and someone should be the leader. I am usually the leader if I am hosting.

Menu ideas

The must-haves are *haroset* and *maror.* These are on the *Seder* plate, but most people will want more of the *haroset* during the meal and the *maror,* or horseradish sauce, which can complement the meat. I usually serve *matzo* ball soup as a first course. For the main meal, we love a good brisket! I make it with carrots, prunes, and onions. Chicken is also a good and less expensive alternative. Some Jews do not eat lamb for this occasion out of respect for the memory of the temple sacrifices. But I have served lamb in the past! If you like it, go for it! We live under grace, so it is acceptable!

We also like noodle *kugel.* Sometimes we also have a spring salad. You will need three pieces of *matzo* for the *afikomen,* and you may want extra for the meal. *Challah* is *not* for this meal as bread must be unleavened!

The Haggadah/the telling

Last year, my aunt Martha Amster Hodges wrote an abbreviated version of the *Haggadah* for our celebration. It has all the elements but takes much less time to do! If you want to do one that has more parts, there are many places you can order *Haggadahs* from, just search online, or see the *appendix 2* for suggestions.

Homemade matzo for Passover

Passover place settings include individual
Seder plate and *Haggadah*

Passover place setting with candies representing the ten plagues

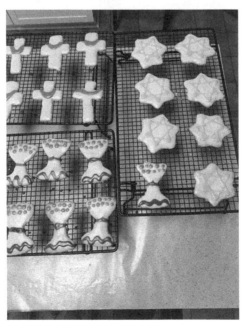

Cookies for Passover include cross, star
of David, cup of Redemption

Passover *Seder* plate centerpiece

Passover *Afikomen* cover, cup for Elijah

Passover place setting with signs for the ten plagues

Passover table with peg people representing the twelve
tribes. Moses is leading them across the Red Sea
while Pharoah is watching from the other side.

CHAPTER 8

Shavuot, Pentecost, Ordinary Time (Part 2)

And you shall observe the Feast of the Harvest of the first
fruits of you labors from what you sow in the field; also
the Feast of the Ingathering at the end of the year when
you gather in the fruit of your labors from the field.
— *Exodus 23:16*

Civic Calendar: Memorial Day—May
Church Calendar: Pentecost, Trinity Sunday—May/June
Ordinary Time: May/June–November
Biblical Calendar: Shavuot—May/June

Passover is a feast that celebrates our redemption. *Shavuot* leads us
to a recommitment for service, obedience, and worship. When the
Israelites left Egypt, they came to Mount Sinai. Exodus 19 relates the
story. "The entire community of Israel camped right in front of the
mountain of God. Moses climbed the mountain to meet with God,
and the Eternal spoke to him from the mountain." The people waited
at the bottom of the mountain for Moses to return and tell them
what God said. It is at this point that God gave what we have come
to call the Ten Commandments. God and the people of Israel were
to enter a covenant agreement. The agreement was this: if they would
do all that the Lord commanded, then his promise to them was to be

their God. "Now if you will hear My voice, obey what I say, and keep my covenant, then you—out of all the nations of the world—will be my treasured people...You will be my kingdom of priests, a nation holy and set apart" (Exodus 19:5). God and the Israelites had entered into a covenant agreement much like a marriage.

The story of Ruth parallels this covenant. In this story, a woman named Naomi, her husband, and two sons left Bethlehem to go to the country of Moab. There, the two sons married Moabite women. All the men died. Naomi and her daughters-in-law began to journey back to Bethlehem. At one point, one of the young women decided to return to Moab. Naomi and Ruth continued the journey together. Along the way, Naomi pleaded with Ruth to return to her own homeland. Ruth refused and said, "Stop pushing me away, insisting that I stop following you! Wherever you go, I will go. Wherever you live, I will live. Your people will be my people. Your God will be my God" (Ruth 1:16). Do you see the similarity between these stories? The Israelites were in the presence of God who spoke through fire and smoke from atop a mountain. They committed themselves to him, they and their children. Ruth, a Gentile, committed herself to a woman of faith and to learning about her God. As a result of the covenant made by the Israelites at Mount Sinai, God gave them instructions, the Law, on how to live and worship him. He promised to be their God and gave them his word. *Shavuot* celebrates the giving of the Torah and the covenant made with God. The story of Ruth is a love story of great commitment, courage, and faith. As a result of Ruth's commitment, she was to become the great-great-grandmother of David whose descendant would be Jesus (Matthew 1). Both of these stories reflect God's presence and provision.[56] God's presence was with the Israelites as they traveled through the wilderness. God's provision was with Naomi and Ruth as his plan unfolded for the coming of his Son.

For me personally, both of these stories reflect my own story. I have Jewish heritage. My son, who took our family name when he was adopted, is now grafted into our story and family. When Glenn and

---

[56] David Brickner, *Christ in the Feast of Tabernacles* (Chicago: Moody Press, 2006), 17.

I were married, his daughters were part of our wedding celebration. They joined us under the *Chupah*, a lace canopy as we committed to become a family together. Our story is certainly not perfect, but we believe it is a reflection of God's plan and provision for all of us!

Shavuot or the Feast of Weeks is also known as Pentecost. Pentecost is the Greek word for "fifty." *Shavuot* begins fifty days after the first night of Passover. Observant Jews will count down the fifty days from Passover to *Shavuot*. This is called "counting the *omer*." An *omer* is a sheaf of wheat or other grain. Deuteronomy chapter 16 gives a few more details about this celebration.

> Another celebration the Eternal your God want you to have is the Feast of Weeks. Hold this celebration seven weeks after you first begin to cut and harvest the barley in your fields. Each of you will choose something to contribute out of what He has blessed you with. Go to the place He chooses for His name; and have a celebration there in His presence with your sons and daughters, you male and female slaves, and the Levites, foreigners, orphans, and widows who live in your city. Remember you were slaves in Egypt, and obey these regulations carefully. (verses 10–12)

When the children of Israel crossed over the Jordan River into the promised land and settled in it by planting fields and building cities, they began to celebrate this festival. When the temple was built in Jerusalem, the people would go up to the temple and present their offerings. This is the last of the three pilgrimage feasts.

Shavuot is a celebration of God's goodness in supplying the physical needs of his people and the spiritual, moral law that they would need as they entered the promised land to build a nation. Tradition says that fifty days after Passover, God gave the Ten Commandments and established a holy covenant with the children of Israel. Today, the celebration mostly focuses on this aspect. This came about as the

Jews were scattered throughout the world through various Diasporas. As they were living in foreign lands, they would have to assimilate to a point. Keeping the Law was difficult, and the pilgrimages to the temple would not have been possible as the temple had been destroyed.

Pentecost was the day that the disciples of Jesus gathered in the Upper Room. Fifty days earlier, Jesus was resurrected from the dead and would later ascend back into heaven. On the fiftieth day, the disciples had gathered in the Upper Room. Acts 2 tells us,

> Suddenly there came from heaven a noise like a violent, rushing wind, and it filled the whole house where they were sitting. And there appeared to them tongues as of fire distributing themselves, and they rested one each one of them. And they were all filled with the Holy Spirit and began to speak with other tongues, as the Spirit was giving them utterance.

The church calendar celebrates Pentecost as the giving of the Holy Spirit. This is the golden thread drawn from the giving of the Law. The two go together as the Law was given as a guide for living, and the Spirit was given to be a helper (John 14:26), a teacher (Luke 12:12), and an enabler for ministry and evangelism (Acts 10:38). The work of the Holy Spirit draws both Jews and Gentiles to the Savior. When the Spirit came upon the disciples, they began to realize that what Jesus had been teaching them all along was that salvation is open to all who believe on him. Just as the *Shavuot* was one of the three pilgrimage feasts where all Jewish men were required to go to Jerusalem and appear before the Lord, so the disciples waited together as Jesus told them to wait for the coming of the Holy Spirit. On this day, the new covenant between God and Israel was enacted (Jeremiah 31:31; Hebrews 9:14, 14).

Like Easter, Pentecost is a huge day for celebration! Churches will decorate with doves depicting the Spirit as it fell on Jesus at his baptism (Matthew 3:13–17). Expressions of fire that represent the flames that appeared on the disciples as they began speaking in other languages (Acts 2) will decorate church sanctuaries. I have seen some incredible decorations at many churches for this day. I recently read that one church begins planning their decor for Pentecost right after Christmas! There are so many creative ways that the church celebrates this momentous day! On this day, we thank God for giving the Holy Spirit to all those who trust in Him. We pray that the Spirit will guide us and direct us in our walk with God. We ask that our eyes, ears, and minds will open to understanding His truth. We ask for courage to live our lives according to his purpose so that others will see the light of Christ in us.

Remember that Pentecost had its roots in *Shavuot*. This is the significance of the two festivals: the giving of the Law and the giving of the Holy Spirit. God gave the Law at Sinai, and he gave the Holy Spirit during Pentecost.

As spring is well under way, and summer is rapidly approaching, foods for the feast represent grains and dairy. This means cheesecake! Homes are decorated with greenery and flowers of the season and represent the Torah as a "tree of life." The Law is compared to milk and honey and is represented in dairy foods. What goes great with milk and honey? Challah bread! Recall that God's Word is often referred to as the Bread of Life. In Leviticus 23, the Lord is telling the Israelites about this feast. The grain offering, or fresh bread, that they are to bring to the Tabernacle was to be made of grain that was freshly harvested. It was to be a wave offering. In Deuteronomy 26, Moses reminded the people how to celebrate this feast. It also included inviting "the foreigners who live in your town." The point was that this feast was to be enjoyed by everyone, regardless of their heritage. The focus is that God meets both our physical as well as our spiritual needs.

> The inclusion of the Gentiles completed the symbolism of the wave offering, where the High Priest offered two loaves of fine wheat flour baked with leaven. Centuries before, the two

loaves of the wave offering symbolized the Body of Messiah made up of both Jewish and Gentile believers. Though the loaves were made of fine wheat flour, they contained leaven, the symbol for sin. That speaks of the fact that the Church, though refined by the blood of the Lamb, still retains the human sin nature until that day when She will be presented as the Bride of Christ, without spot or wrinkle.[57]

Decorations

As mentioned, greenery and seasonal flowers make for an inviting and beautiful table. Use fresh cuts from your garden! If the weather is nice, why not have your celebration meal outside, picnic style! This year, the weather was not as warm as I would have liked in order to eat outside, but I did use some very floral paper plates and matching napkins. I placed a sheaf of wheat (that also comes out at Thanksgiving time) along with an arrangement of silk flowers and greens. I also made two loaves of fresh challah wrapped in a special challah cover. These two loaves, braided with six strands each, represent Jew and Gentile believers in community together.

Menu ideas

On our menu this year was falafels with pita. I made three different spreads for the pita and stuffed them with lettuce, tomatoes, and cucumbers. The spreads were hummus, made from chickpeas, Tzatziki, a Greek dill sauce, and Tahini, Israeli sesame butter. A Mediterranean salad, mushroom, and cheese blintzes were served. And the yummiest halva cheesecake with berries and cream were our dessert!

---

[57] www.jewsforjesus.org, (Accessed 5.22.2020).

Liturgy

Enjoying the food and fellowship around your table is so rewarding! But let's remember what it is we are celebrating and also use it as a way to tell more of God's story to each other and worship Him. I created a brief liturgy to help my family and guests in their remembrance and thankfulness. Psalm 67 is traditionally used because, in Hebrew, there are only forty-nine words in the Psalm! I also assign readings to my guests so they also get to participate!

See *appendix 2* for the full liturgy.

The Sunday after Pentecost is Trinity Sunday. This day focuses on the unique three persons of the Trinity. It is important to be reminded that our faith is triune. Unlike other religions or belief systems, Christians believe that God is Father, Son, and Holy Spirit. We are made in the image of God and the "significance of Christian community that mirrors the eternal, communal relationship."[58]

The following weeks are Ordinary Time. Whew! What a year it has been! The summer months are time for a more relaxed pace and a focus on growing in our Christian faith and understanding of who God is in our lives. On the church calendar, Ordinary Time continues until Christ the King Sunday—the Sunday before Advent. The biblical calendar continues until the New Year begins on *Rosh Hashanah*.

And so we have celebrated, feasted, and learned about the biblical convocations that God set forth for his people to remember. His story helps each person see, feel, taste, and enjoy a place within his story. The telling of God's story helps each of us know him more. I think of both my parents and all my grandparents who have long left this earth. How I wish I knew them better! What I remember from my childhood is important, but it is also important for me to hear stories from other relatives who knew them longer than I did. I do

---

[58] Robert E. Webber. Ancient-Future Time: Forming Spirituality through the Christian Year. (Grand Rapids, MI: Baker Books, 2004), 175.

have papers and letters that I can also read and glean insights into their lives. Doing all of this helps me understand myself better and how I fit into my family. So it is with how we learn about being in God's family. We read his Word; we memorize it and hide it in our hearts. We hear it from pastors and teachers, and we share it with others. Just as Jesus said, He is the vine, and we are the branches (John 14:1–5). We are grafted into him, into his family. As we live and move and are part of the family of God, we become more like him.

Like I said, it has been a very crazy year! As I finish up this writing, we are months into the COVID-19 pandemic. It has had a real impact in all of our lives this year. Most people have shut themselves up at home, hoarded toilet paper and yeast, and stayed home from most all activities including church. For me, a lot of my activities have been curtailed or canceled. We have tried to be as "normal" as possible. All of this has impacted our family activities to varying degrees.

Jesus said, "Don't get lost in despair, believe in God, and keep on believing in me" (John 14:1). Dear reader, this is how we maneuver through these crazy days! Pray that Messiah will come again and soon! Until then, hold steady in your faith; pray without ceasing. Trust and know that God is in control and sovereign over all.

It has been my desire to write this book for several years now. It has taken me almost a year and a half to complete! My family has been celebrating the festivals for more than twenty years. We started with *Hanukkah* and Passover, and then as I began to research more, we added the others to our yearly routine. As I stated at the beginning, we do not always do everything on the exact date. Sometimes even birthdays, anniversaries, and other special events get shifted because of scheduling. We give each other lots of grace just as God gives us grace to do what we can when we are able. For us, most years, even our Christmas celebrations happen a day or more later than December 25. It is okay, and we have learned to adapt. The same goes for the biblical feasts. If you are going to include more family members and friends, it is a good practice to start planning early so that everyone has time to get schedules arranged.

If you are just starting to put any of these festivals into your practice, may I suggest you start with one or two and go from there! Remember that growing in faith is a lot like watching a baby grow and develop. First comes crawling, then standing, taking first steps, and so on. It is the same when we first become Christ followers. We learn and grow in faith by putting into practice the things we learn by reading, studying the Word, and being in fellowship with other Christ followers.

The recipes and liturgies that follow are references for you. Well, really, they are for me! I wanted a place to keep all of these in one place for easy reference! If they help you, that's an added blessing to me! All of the recipes have been tried, tested, and eaten at my table or Aunt Martha's table. So we know they are really good! The liturgies have also been used, revised, and rewritten. Please use them as you like or develop your own. The point is to help us all in our faith journey in knowing the Eternal One more!

And now, "May the Eternal One bless and keep you. May He make His face shine upon you and be gracious to you. The Eternal lift up His countenance to look upon you and give you peace" (Numbers 6:24–26).

Shalom!

Shavuot décor with menorah and torah scroll

Shavuot place setting with torah scroll, liturgy inside

Shavuot décor

Shavuot centerpiece

Moses and the ten commandments atop Mt. Sinai

Shavuot centerpiece

Shavuot lamb kabobs, mushroom and
cheese blintzes, Jerusalem bagel

Shavuot desserts—kunafeh and chocolate halva cheesecake

APPENDIX 1

The Recipes

You may notice that several of the recipes are listed more than once. That is because I use them for more than one feast. The recipes are organized by feast with menu suggestions. Feel free to mix and match as you like and depending on where you live and what is available at your local grocers.

Rosh Hashanah/Yom Kippur

Dinner menu

> *Appetizers*
> Apples and honey, assorted dried fruits
> Pomegranate and honey-glazed chicken
> Spinach vegetable kugel
> Couscous salad
> Challah (round)
>
> *Dessert*
> Honey spice cake
> Kunafeh

Pomegranate Honey-Glazed Chicken

4 lbs. of boneless chicken breasts, cut in half
4 T. oil, separated
1 large onion, chopped
3 cloves garlic, minced
1/2 c. pomegranate molasses
1/2 c. sweetened pomegranate juice
1/2 c. honey
2 c. vegetable or chicken broth
1 t. cumin
1/2 t. powdered ginger
1/8 t. allspice
1/2 t. turmeric
Salt and pepper to taste
Garnish with 2 t. chopped, fresh parsley and 2 t. pomegranate seeds

1. Heat 2 tablespoons oil in a large pan.
2. Sauté chopped onion until soft and translucent. Add minced garlic and sauce for 2–3 minutes; do not brown!
3. Add pomegranate molasses, juice, honey, broth, and spices to onion/garlic mixture.
4. Stir and bring to a boil. Reduce heat to an active simmer; cook uncovered of about 20 minutes or until sauce is reduced by about 1/2 and slightly thickened.
5. Taste and adjust seasoning. If too tart, add more honey. Add more pepper for more kick!
6. Rinse chicken parts and pat dry. Season with salt and pepper.
7. Heat 2 tablespoons oil in another skillet and place chicken parts skin side down. If using skinless parts, pick a side! Brown on one side and flip over to brown the other side. Do not crowd chicken as it won't brown properly!
8. Lower heat; pour prepared sauce over chicken. Cover pan, and simmer on low for 35–40 minutes.

9. Remove from pan to serving platter. Garnish with chopped parsley and pomegranate seeds.

Serves 8.

This is a really yummy way to serve chicken! I happen to have a friend with a pomegranate tree, so I can get them from her when they are truly ripe! How to tell if a pomegranate is ripe? It should look all wrinkly and even be splitting! Not the beautiful red perfectly round that you get at the local market!

Spinach Vegetable Kugel

1 bunch fresh spinach
2 small onions, chopped
1 stalk celery
1 red bell pepper, chopped
3 carrots, grated
1 c. mushrooms, chopped
1 T. olive oil
2 eggs
1/4 t. garlic powder
1/4 t. black pepper
1/2 t. dried basil
1/4 c. matzo meal

1. Preheat oven to 350 degrees. Wash spinach thoroughly; remove and discard tough stems. Cook spinach in a covered saucepan until wilted, about 3 minutes. Do not add any water as the water that is still on the leaves will provide enough to steam it. Cool and squeeze dry.
2. Heat oil in skillet on medium heat. Sauté onion, celery, red pepper, and carrots for 5 minutes until golden.
3. Add mushrooms and cook 5 minutes longer.

4. Chop spinach coarsely. Combine with remaining ingredients and mix well. Pour into a sprayed 8×10-inch casserole.
5. Bake uncovered for 45–50 minutes, until firm. Cut into squares to serve.

Makes 6 servings.

Quick and Easy Challah

For two loaves

2 T. quick-rise yeast
2 c. warm water
1 T. salt
1/4 c. plus 2 T. sugar (you can substitute honey or even date syrup!)
1/2 c. (one cube) butter
2 eggs
6–7 c. flour
Olive oil and a little extra flour

1. Line baking sheet with parchment.
2. Sprinkle yeast over warm water in stand mixing bowl (not metal) using whisk. Mix gently to blend yeast in. Stir in salt, sugar (honey or syrup), and 2 eggs; beat well. Gradually mix in flour, one cup at a time, up to 7 cups, until dough is tacky but not wet. After about 4 cups of the flour, change to dough hook. Knead with dough hook for about 5 minutes. Turn dough out onto surface to knead or, if using a mixer, knead on high for a few minutes.
3. Depending on your work surface, use either flour or oil to knead the dough by hand a few times.
4. Cut dough in half with pastry cutter. Knead one lump a few times using hands to elongate into about a footlong roll. Cut in half, and then cut each half into three smaller

pieces. You now have 6 small balls. Using your hands, roll each ball into a footlong strand. Pinch all strands together at the top and braid. When you get to the bottom, fold the last bit under for a nice finish. Repeat for remaining loaf.

5. Place loaves on parchment-lined baking sheet. Cover with a tea towel, and let rise about 60 minutes or until double in size.

   (I have been putting my loaves in bread pans sprayed with oil so they rise higher and can be used for sandwiches later in the week.)

6. Whisk one more egg in ramekin with 1 tablespoon of water and brush the tops of loaves with pastry brush.

7. Bake in preheated 350-degree oven for 30–35 minutes or until tops are golden brown. During the last 10 minutes of baking, brush tops with what's left of the egg-wash and finish baking

8. Let cool before slicing (if you can wait that long!)

I make this almost every week! There are many videos online about braiding. This is a basic recipe that can also be used for making rolls. Look for videos online to get ideas how to shape into rolls and other kinds of braids. On Yom Kippur, challah should be formed into round, crown-shaped loaves. The purpose of having six strands in your bread and making two loaves is that each strand represents a tribe of Israel. So with two loaves, you have a total of twelve strands representing the twelve tribes of Israel!

Sangria

1/2 c. honey
1 pomegranate
1 apple, cored and sliced thin
12 oz. seedless grapes
1 bottle red wine, Syrah or Shiraz works well!
2 c. pure 100% pomegranate juice
1 c. grape juice

1/4 brandy
1/4 triple sec

1. Pour honey and 1/2 cup water into a small saucepan. Heat over medium heat stirring constantly until honey is completely dissolved into the water. Do not let it boil!
2. Remove from heat and allow to cool. This is the honey simple syrup.
3. Seed pomegranate. Discard the rind and pith.
4. Place pomegranate seed into the bottom of large pitcher.
5. Place apples on top of the seeds.
6. Place grapes on top of the apple slices.
7. Pour the lentil bottle of wine into pitcher.
8. Add pomegranate juice, grape juice, brandy, triple sec, and honey syrup into the pitcher. Stir gently with long-handled wooden spoon to blend all flavors together.
9. Chill in refrigerator for at least 2 hours before serving. Stir again before serving.

Serves 8.

You could leave out the brandy and triple sec if you don't have these on hand. I don't and I would not notice the difference!

Kunafeh (also spelled Knafeh, Kanafeh)

10.5 oz. Kataifi pastry (purchase online or at a Middle Eastern shop)
1 1/2 c. butter, melted
10.5 oz. mozzarella
9 oz. mascarpone
1 c. rose-scented simple syrup
3 T coarsely chopped pistachios
1–2 T dried, edible rose petals

Rose-Scented Simple Syrup

1 c. water
1 1/4 c. sugar
1 t. fresh lemon juice
2 T. rose water/orange blossom water

Day before

Make simple syrup

1. Place the water and sugar in a saucepan and let it come to a boil.
2. Lower heat and simmer for 5 minutes to thicken.
3. Remove from heat, and stir in lemon juice and rose water.
4. Cool to room temperature, and then place in refrigerator until the next day.

Mozzarella

1. Cut into slices and soak in plenty of cool water in a large bowl. Place in refrigerator overnight, and change the water at least a handful of times. The water will get cloudy.

Baking day

1. Preheat oven to 375 degrees.
2. Place Kataifi in a food processor and pulse a few times until the pastry is all shredded.
3. Place the shredded pastry in a large bowl and pour most of the melted butter, and reserve some for later.
4. Using your fingers, mix it all thoroughly coating all strands of pastry with the butter.
5. Add the rest of the butter if needed; mix thoroughly again, and set aside as you get ready to work on the cheese.

6. Clean food processor, and place the drained mozzarella in.
7. Blitz the mozzarella into a large bowl, and add the mascarpone.
8. Using a wooden spoon, beat the two cheeses together until thoroughly combined.

Assembly

1. Place half the butter-soaked pastry into the bottom of a glass pan, and pat down firmly.
2. Top with the cheese mixture.
3. Top the cheese with the other half of the pastry and pat down firmly but gently so that the cheese does not get displaced.
4. Place onion the middle of the preheated oven and bake for 35–40 minutes until the pastry is a lovely golden shade.
5. Let cool for 5 minutes, then using a butter knife, run it through the sides of the knife to release any pastry and cheese that might be sticking to the sides of the dish.
6. Place a serving plate over the baking dish and invert onto the serving plate.
7. Pour the cold syrup all over the knife until it is saturated with the syrup and is shiny all over. Reserve some for serving.
8. Leave to cool for 10 minutes, then using a sharp knife, cut into little squares.
9. Garnish with the pistachios and rose petals.
10. Serve with the leftover syrup in a little pitcher.

Makes about 20 squares.

This is truly a work of art and is quite delish! It is reminiscent of baklava. I would put the recipe for the pastry here, but we found that it was much easier to purchase it. Plus, it saved quite a bit of time as this recipe is time-consuming! You can also purchase the rose water and orange water at a Middle Eastern market or online. We found a Middle Eastern market in our area and made a visit. It was an experience! The shopkeeper was most helpful and even gave us some samples to taste!

Honey Spice Cake

2 c. sugar

2 1/2 t. baking powder

1 1/2 t. ground cinnamon

1/2 t. baking soda

1/4 t. ground cloves

1/4 t. ground nutmeg

1/8 t. salt

3/4 c. unsweetened applesauce

2 eggs

1/4 c. canola oil

1/4 c. honey

1/4 c. finely chopped walnuts, toasted

Ganache

1/4 c. dark chocolate chips

3 T. heavy whipping cream

1. In a large bowl, combine the first 8 ingredients. Whisk the applesauce, eggs, oil, and honey in separate bowl. Stir wet ingredients into dry ingredients just until moistened. Fold in walnuts.
2. Spray a 9-inch square baking dish with cooking spray, and pour mixture into the dish. Bake at 350 degrees for 15–20 minutes or until a toothpick inserted in the middle comes out clean. Cool completely on a wire rack.
3. For ganache, place chips in a small bowl. In the microwave, heat cream for 20–30 seconds or just until bubbly. Pour

over chocolate; whisk until smooth. Cool slightly, then drizzle over the cake.

Serves 9 or so.

This is an easy and quick recipe that is just yummy!

Sukkot

Dinner menu

> Meatballs with mushroom sauce
> Maple-glazed carrots
> Israeli couscous tabouleh

Dessert
Apple-pear strudel

Meatballs with Mushroom Sauce

Mushroom sauce

> 2 lb. mushrooms, sliced
> 2–4 T. olive oil
> 1–2 t. kosher salt
> 4 c. milk
> 2 T. soy sauce
> 1 c. cream

To make the sauce

1. Lightly sauté the mushrooms in oil and salt.
2. Add the milk and bring to boil. Simmer for 1/2 hour.
3. Add the cream and soy sauce, and simmer a few more minutes.

Meatballs

> 2 lb. ground beef
> 1/2 c. breadcrumbs
> 1/2 c. water or mild

1/2 onion, finely diced
2 cloves garlic, crushed
1 t. kosher salt
Pinch of basil
Pinch of oregano

1. Put the breadcrumbs and water (or milk) into a small bowl for 10 minutes until soggy. Gently mix the wet bread-crumbs with the rest of the meatball ingredients until just combined.
2. Roll the meat mixture into every sized balls, and drop into the gently simmering sauce. Cook; cover for 20 minutes until cooked through. Do not overcook or cook on too high, or meatballs will fall apart.
3. Serve over rice, orzo, or couscous. Garnish with fresh herbs.

If you don't have enough time for all this, use premade frozen meatballs!

Maple-Glazed Carrots

12 medium carrots
2 T. olive oil
2 T. orange juice
Grated zest from one small orange
1 t. salt
2 t. nutmeg
2 T. apple juice concentrate
1 T. maple syrup or extract

1. Peel the carrots and slice into 1/4 inch pieces. Place carrots in a covered vegetable steamer over boiling water for 10 minutes or until tender. Remove from heat and set aside.

2. Heat the oil in a large saucepan. Add orange juice, orange zest, steamed carrots, salt, nutmeg, and apple juice concentrate. Stir to coat until heated through.
3. Remove from heat, and add maple syrup; mix well.
4. Serve immediately.

Simple, yet really tasty!

Couscous Tabouleh

1 1/2 c. pearl couscous
1 c. chicken broth
3/4 c. water
1/2 c. fresh lemon juice, divided
2 1/2 t. kosher salt, divided
1/3 c. seeded cucumber cut into 1/4" pieces
2 c. cherry tomatoes cut in half
1 c. minced scallions, white and green parts
1 1/2 c. loosely packed fresh parsley, minced
1 c. loosely packed fresh mint, minced plus some mint sprigs for garnish.

1. In a saucepan, combine the broth, water, 1/4 cup lemon juice and 1 1/2 teaspoon salt. Bring to a boil, and stir in the couscous. Cover and let couscous simmer for 10 minutes.
2. In a large bowl, stir together cucumber, tomatoes, scallion, olive oil, and remaining 1/4 teaspoon salt. Let mixture stand for 15 minutes. Add the couscous, parsley, and mint. Stir the salad well. Chill; cover for an hour.
3. The salad may be made up to 2 days in advance. Keep covered and chilled. Garnish with mint sprigs before serving.

Serve 4.

Apple-Pear Strudel

2 sheets frozen puff pastry
2 medium-large apples, peeled and finely diced
2 large, ripe Bosc pears, peeled and finely diced
1/2 c. raisins, or Craisins
1/4 c. chopped walnuts
1/4 c. sugar
1 t. ground cinnamon to taste
2 t. lemon juice

1. Allow puff pastry to thaw for 45 minutes up to an hour. Turn the sheets of puff pastry onto a parchment-lined baking sheet.
2. Preheat oven to 375 degrees.
3. Combine all ingredients in a large mixing bowl, and stir together to cover mixture with the cinnamon and sugar.
4. Divide the apple-pear mixture in half between the two sheets of puff pastry. Spread evenly to the edges leaving a one-inch strip at the end furthest from you.
5. Roll up, jellyroll style, starting the side closest to you. The roll should end up seam-side down.
6. Make 7 shallow slits crosswise at even intervals, so you have 8 slices on each roll.
7. Bake in preheated oven for 25–30 minutes or until golden and puffed.
8. Remove from oven and transfer to racks to cool.

Serve warm or at room temperature with ice cream or whipped cream or make a glaze of powdered sugar and a little almond extract to drizzle over.

Hanukkah

Dinner menu

Potato latkes
Brisket with carrot tzimmes
3-apple applesauce, sour cream
Green salad (optional)
Pecan noodle kugel (or other kind of kugel)

Dessert
Decorated sugar cookies
Hanukkah sufganiyot (jelly-filled doughnuts)

Breakfast menu

Cheese blintzes
Winter fruit salad
Challah

Potato Latke Casserole with Cranberry Applesauce

6–8 Yukon gold potatoes
1 white or yellow onion
2 T. flour
2 eggs
1 t. salt
1/2 t. cumin
2 T. olive oil
Paprika and fresh pepper for sprinkling
1 T. oil for drizzling
Cranberry applesauce and sour cream for serving

1. Using a grater or food processor fitted with the grating blade, grate potatoes and onion.

2. Transfer potato/onion mixture to a colander lined with a thin dishtowel and ring out all the excess liquid. Squeeze hard and get as much liquid out as you can! This will make it all the crispier!

3. In a large bowl, whisk the egg, flour, salt, and cumin. Add the drained potato/onion mixture and mix well to combine.

4. Spread 2 tablespoons of oil in a casserole dish (9x9) for a thicker casserole or 8x13 for a thinner, crisper casserole; warm in the oven for 2 minutes. Remove from oven and transfer the mixture into the dish. Drizzle with the remaining tablespoon of oil and sprinkle generously with paprika and fresh ground pepper.

5. Bake for 1 hour or until casserole is nicely browned.

Meanwhile, make the cranberry applesauce (can also be done ahead of time).

Cranberry Applesauce

5–6 of your favorite sweet apples, any combination tastes great! Peel and chop roughly.
1 c. fresh cranberries
1 stick of cinnamon or 1/2 t. ground cinnamon
1–2 T. white sugar
3/4 c. water
Juice from 1/2 lemon *or* about 2 T. lemon from concentrate

1. Combine all ingredients except lemon juice in a medium saucepan. Bring to a boil, and then reduce to a simmer.

2. Cover and cook for 30–40 minutes or until desired consistency is reached. Stir often to avoid sticking.

3. Remove from heat and stir in lemon juice.

4. Mash apples and cranberries with potato masher until desired consistency.

Serves 6–8.

To serve casserole, cut into squares and top with cranberry applesauce and/or sour cream. This is best when served warm, right out of the oven!

Three-Apple Applesauce

2 c. water
1/2 c. fresh lemon juice
3 lb. Fuji apples or other sweet apples
3 lb. Granny Smith apples or other tart apples
3 lb. Jonathan or Rome Beauty apples or other soft-textured apples
2 1/4 c. sugars
1 1/2 t. coarse kosher salt
1/2 t. ground cinnamon
1/2 t. ground allspice

1. Combine 2 cups of water and lemon juice in a 10–12-quart stockpot.
2. Peel, core, and cut apples into small pieces. Mix pieces into lemon water as soon as apples are cut to prevent browning.
3. Add sugar, coarse salt, cinnamon, and allspice. Stir over medium-high heat until sugar dissolves.
4. Bring to a boil; reduce heat, cover, and simmer until apples are soft and almost translucent, stirring frequently about 20 minutes.
5. Remove from heat. Using a potato masher, mash apples into desired consistency.
6. Ladle applesauce into hot, clean 1-pint glass canning jars, leave about 1-inch headroom at top of jars. *
7. Remove air bubbles. Wipe jar threads and rims with damp cloth. Cover with hot lids; apply screw bands. Process jars in pot of boiling water for 20 minutes. Cool jars completely. Store in cool dark place up to 1 year.

Makes 6–7 1-pint jars.

I use the plastic canning jars that I purchase online. These work great! Then I freeze my applesauce until I want to use it.

Pecan Noodle Kugel

1 16 oz. package broad egg noodles
4 eggs
1/4 c. melted butter, divided
1 c. brown sugar, divided
1 pinch salt
1/2 c. chopped pecans

1. Fill a large pot with lightly salted water and bring to a rolling boil over high heat. Once the water is boiling, stir in noodles and return to boil.
2. Cook noodles uncovered, stirring occasionally until noodles have cooked through for about 5 minutes. Drain well in a colander set in the sink.
3. Preheat oven to 325 degrees.
4. Beat egg in a large bowl. Beat in half of the melted butter, and then stir in 1 cup of the brown sugar and pinch of salt.
5. Stir in the noodles, making sure noodles get evenly coated.
6. Spread the remaining butter on the bottom of a casserole dish. Sprinkle remaining cup of brown sugar in the casserole dish, patting the sugar up the sides. Spread pecans over the brown sugar. Pour noodle mixture over the sugar/pecans.
7. Bake in preheated oven until firm for about 1 hour and 15 minutes. Run a knife between the *kugel* and the edge of the baking dish. Hold the pan on its side and gently tap the sides of the dish against the counter to loosen it.
8. Cover the dish with a large platter and invert it to tip the *kugel* out of the baking dish and onto the platter.

Serves 8.

This is the best kugel! You will want to eat it at every event!

Crispy Potato Latkes

4 large Russet potatoes
1 yellow onion
1 egg, beaten
1 t. salt
2 T. all-purpose flour
Ground black pepper to taste
2 c. oil for frying

1. Finely grate potatoes and onion into a large bowl. Drain off any excess liquid. The drier the better!
2. Mix in egg, salt, and black pepper. Add enough flour to make mixture thick, about 2–4 tablespoons altogether.
3. Turn oven onto low, about 200 degrees.
4. Heat 1/4 inch of oil in the bottom of a heavy skillet over medium-high heat. Drop two or three mounds of potato mixture into hot oil and flatten to make 1/2 inch thick pancake. Pancakes should be about 2–3 inches in diameter for crispier results!
5. Fry, turning once, until golden brown. Transfer to paper towel-lined plate to drain. Add paper towels for each batch to keep them from sticking to each other.
6. Keep warm in the oven until serving time. Repeat until all latke mixture is used.

Serves 8.

Potato latkes can be made a day ahead! I put mine in a glass baking dish after they are all made, wrap with foil and refrigerate until about 1 hour before serving. Place in 350-degree oven to reheat.

Beef Brisket with Prunes and Merlot

This recipe is my go-to for both Passover and Hanukkah.

For 8 servings

4 4 1/2 lb. flat-cut beef brisket, trimmed
2 T. olive oil
1 14 1/2 oz. can diced tomatoes in juice
1 c. Merlot or other dry red wine
2 lb. red onions, sliced
4 medium-sized carrots, peeled and thinly sliced
16 garlic cloves, peeled
1 1/2 c. pitted large prunes (about 8 oz.)
1 T. finely chopped thyme
1/2 c. plus 1 T. prune juice
3 T. plus 1 t. balsamic vinegar
2 T. chopped fresh Italian parsley
Salt and pepper to taste

1. Position rack in bottom third of oven and preheat to 325 degrees F. Pat brisket dry; sprinkle all over with salt and pepper.
2. Heat oil in heavy extra-large skillet over high heat. Add brisket and cook until deep brown, about 7 minutes per side.
3. Transfer brisket, fat side up, to large roasting pan. Add tomatoes with juice and wine to skillet. Remove from heat; scrape up any browned bits, and pour mixture over brisket.
4. Distribute onions, carrots, and garlic around brisket. Add prunes and thyme; drizzle with 1/2 cup prune juice and 3 tablespoon vinegar. Sprinkle with salt and pepper.
5. Place pan over 2 burners and bring to boil. Cover pan with heavy-duty foil; place in oven.

6. Braise brisket until tender, about 3 hours and 15 minutes. Uncover and cool 1 hour, or so, at room temperature.

   This can be made up to 2 days ahead of time and will save a lot of work on your special day! Cover with foil and chill. Bring just to simmer over 2 burners before continuing.

7. Remove brisket from roasting pan, scraping off juices. Place on work surface; cut across grain into 1/4-inch-thick slices. Spoon off fat from top of pan juices. Place 1 cup vegetables (no prunes) and 1 cup braising liquid from pan into processor and puree. Return pure to pan. Add remaining 1 tablespoon prune juice and 1 teaspoon vinegar to pan. Heat sauce; season with salt and pepper.

8. Overlap brisket slices in 13×9× 2-inch glass baking dish. Pour sauce over brisket, separating slices to allow some sauce to flow between. *This can be done 1 day ahead! Cover; chill.*

9. Rewarm brisket, covered, in 350-degree F oven for 30 minutes. Sprinkle brisket with parsley; serve.

Brisket Overnight

3 onions
3 whole heads of garlic, sliced in half to reveal the cloves
1 whole brisket
Kosher salt
Freshly cracked black pepper
1 c. dry red wine
3 c. beef or chicken broth
1 c. crushed tomatoes (optional)

1. Preheat oven to 225 degrees.
2. Layer sliced onions and garlic in a large roasting pan or Dutch oven. Season brisket with salt and pepper.

3. Place brisket on top of onions and garlic. Pour red wine, broth, and tomatoes, if using, into pan. Cover food directly with a layer of parchment, and then seal tightly with foil.

4. Roast in oven at 225 for 10 hours.

5. Carefully transfer brisket to a cutting board to cool before slicing. While brisket is cooling, strain onions and garlic from pan juices. Press onions and garlic so that all juices run out. Skim fat off of pan juices and reduce pan juices on the stovetop until it coats the back of a spoon.

6. Slice brisket across the grain and transfer back to braising pan. Store in refrigerator for up to 3 days or freeze for up to one month. Freeze juices separately.

7. Reheat brisket, covered, in a low oven at 250 degrees until hot. Serve with warmed, reduced pan juices.

Hanukkah/Passover Cookies

Sugar Cookies

1 1/2 c. butter, softened
2 c. white sugar
4 eggs
1 t. vanilla
5 c. all-purpose flour
2 t. baking powder
1 t. salt

1. In a bowl of stand mixer, cream together butter and sugar until smooth. Beat in eggs and vanilla. Stir in flour, one cup at a time, baking powder, and salt. Cover and chill dough for at least an hour or overnight.
2. Preheat oven to 400 degrees. Roll out dough on floured surface 1/4–1/2 inch thick. Use Star of David and *Dreidel* cookie cutters* to cut shapes. Place cookies 1 inch apart on ungreased baking sheets.
3. Bake 6–8 minutes in preheated oven. Cool completely before frosting.

For Passover, I use a cross, Star of David, cup of redemption, and Torah-shaped cookie cutters. For Hanukkah, I use Star of David—the cup of redemption cutter can be used for a menorah—and a Dreidel cutter.

Sugar Cookie Frosting

1 c. confectioners' sugar
2 t. milk
2 t. light corn syrup
1/4 t. almond extract

1. In a small bowl, stir together confectioners' sugar and milk until smooth. Beat in corn syrup and almond extract until icing is smooth and glossy. If it is too thick, add more corn syrup.
2. Divide into separate bowls or icing tubes with small tips. Add blue food color to one bowl, and mix a few drops of yellow and green to make brown. Leave one white for background color. Use a pastry brush to paint white icing onto stars and dreidel-shaped cookies. When they are dried, pipe blue icing onto stars, overlapping two triangles to make a Star of David. Use the brown color to pipe the traditional letters for the *Dreidel* game onto the *Dreidel*-shaped cookies.

Refer back to chapter 4 for instructions for playing the Dreidel game.

These cookies are just so good! I think the secret is the almond flavoring in the icing. These cookies can also be made for Pentecost/Sukkot using the Star of David, Torah, and dove shapes. Decorate as elaborately as you like!

Hanukkah Jelly-Filled Doughnuts (Sufaniyot)

This is a fun recipe to make with children! Let them do some of the steps by themselves!

1 pkg. dry yeast
4 T. sugar
3/4 c. lukewarm milk
2 1/2 c. all-purpose flour
Pinch of salt
1 t. ground cinnamon
2 eggs, separated
2 T. butter, softened

Strawberry or apricot preserves, whatever your favorite is!
Sugar
Vegetable oil for deep-frying

1. Mix together the yeast, 2 tablespoons of sugar and milk. Let sit until it bubbles.
2. Sift flour and mix with the remaining sugar, salt, cinnamon, egg yolks, and yeast mixture.
3. Knead dough until it forms a ball. Add butter. Knead some more until the butter is well-absorbed. Cover with a towel and let rise overnight in the refrigerator.
4. Roll out the dough to about 1/8-inch thick.
5. Cut out the dough into 24 rounds with a small juice glass or any object about 2 inches in diameter.
6. Place 1/2 teaspoon of preserves in the center of 12 of the rounds. Top with the other 12 rounds and press edges down to form the doughnut. Seal edges with egg whites.
7. Crimp edges with your thumb and finger. Let rise for 30 minutes.
8. Heat 2 inches of oil to about 375 degrees. Drop the doughnuts into the hot oil, a few at a time. Turn to brown on both sides. Drain on paper towels.
9. Roll doughnuts in sugar and enjoy!

Cheese Blintzes

For crepes

This is my mother's recipe that I have used forever!

3/4 c. flour
3 eggs
1 c. milk
1 t. vanilla
Butter

1. Beat eggs in a bowl of stand mixer. Gradually add flour and milk, alternating. Add vanilla and mix well to combine all ingredients.
2. Melt 1 tablespoon butter in skillet, per crepe. Pour enough batter into pan just to thinly cover the bottom of the skillet. When bottom is lightly browned, flip crepe over using a wide spatula. Brown other side.
3. Scoop crepe out of pan with spatula onto plate. Place a paper towel between each crepe so that they don't get all stuck together before filling!

Crepes can be made ahead of time and refrigerated or frozen.

For filling

1 1/2 c. farmers cheese (substitutes are ricotta, queso blanco, or neufchâtel)
2 c. cottage cheese
1/4 c. sugar
1 1/2 t. ground cinnamon
1 T. all-purpose flour

1. In a food processor, blend cheese, sugar, and cinnamon until smooth. Add flour, if necessary, to thicken.
2. Preheat oven to 250 degrees. Line a baking sheet with parchment.
3. Put 3 tablespoons of filling in center of each pancake and fold opposite sides over filling until sides barely touch. Fold ends to in to completely enclose filling, forming a packet. Arrange on baking sheet, seam side down. Use same technique to teach blintz.
4. Bake blintzes, covered loosely with foil. Heat through 5–10 minutes. Serve immediately.

Winter Fruit Salad

Apples
Bananas
Pear
Oranges
Persimmons
Craisins
Walnuts (optional but a must in my family)
Dates, chopped
Parsley *or* cilantro
Dressing

Use any fruits that are in season. Depending on how many people you are serving will determine how many of each fruit. For a family of four, I would use one of each.

1. Dice fruit into small pieces.
2. Mix all fruit together.
3. Toss with dressing.

Dressing

1 large spoonful of mayonnaise
1 large spoonful of honey
Cinnamon

Mix mayonnaise and honey together in small bowl. Sprinkle in some honey and mix together. Depending on how much fruit you have used will determine how much mayo and honey you need. I never measure this; just go by "feel!" Toss into the fruit. It should just glaze the fruit, not overwhelm it!

This is my secret sauce *recipe!*

Challah bread, each having six strands

Quick and Easy Challah

For two loaves

2 T. quick-rise yeast
2 c. warm water
1 T. salt
1/4 c. plus 2 T. sugar (you can substitute honey or even date syrup!)
1/2 c. (one cube) butter
2 eggs
6–7 c. flour
Olive oil and a little extra flour

1. Line baking sheet with parchment.
2. Sprinkle yeast over warm water in stand mixing bowl (not metal) using whisk. Mix gently to blend yeast in. Stir in salt,

sugar (honey or syrup), and 2 eggs; beat well. Gradually mix in flour, one cup at a time, up to 7 cups until dough is tacky but not wet. After about 4 cups of the flour, change to dough hook. Knead with dough hook for about 5 minutes. Turn dough out onto surface to knead or, if using a mixer, knead on high for a few minutes.

3. Depending on your work surface, use either flour or oil to knead the dough by hand a few times.

4. Cut dough in half with pastry cutter. Knead one lump a few times using hands to elongate into about a footlong roll. Cut in half and then cut each half into three smaller pieces. You now have 6 small balls. Using your hands, roll each ball into a footlong strand. Pinch all strands together at the top and braid. When you get to the bottom, fold the last bit under for a nice finish. Repeat for remaining loaf.

5. Place loaves on parchment-lined baking sheet. Cover with a tea towel and let rise about 60 minutes or until double in size.

    I have been putting my loaves in bread pans sprayed with oil so they rise higher and can be used for sandwiches later in the week.

6. Whisk one more egg in ramekin with 1 tablespoon of water and brush the tops of loaves with pastry brush.

7. Bake in preheated 350-degree oven for 30–35 minutes or until tops are golden brown. During the last 10 minutes of baking, brush tops with what's left of the egg wash and finish baking.

8. Let cool before slicing. (If you can wait that long!)

I make this almost every week! There are many videos online about braiding. This is a basic recipe that can also be used for making rolls. Look for videos online to get ideas how to shape into rolls and other kinds of braids. On Yom Kippur, challah should be formed into round crown-shaped loaves. The purpose of having 6 strands in your bread and making 2 loaves is that each strand represents a tribe of Israel. So with 2 loaves, you have a total of 12 strands representing the 12 tribes of Israel!

A Sweet Challah

1 T. active dry yeast
1/3 c. white sugar
2 c. warm water
3 c. all-purpose flour
4 eggs
1/2 c. oil
1 T. salt
1 c. white sugar
6 c. all-purpose flour
1 egg
1 t. oil
2 t. white sugar
1 t. water

1. Mix yeast, 1/3 cup sugar, and warm water together in large bowl of stand mixer. Blend to dissolve the sugar and let mixture stand until a creamy layer forms on top, about 5 minutes. (Don't rush it!) Stir in 3 cups of flour to make a loose sponge.
2. In another bowl, beat 4 eggs, 1/2 cup oil, 1 tablespoon salt, and 1 cup of sugar together. Stir egg mixture into the yeast-flour mixture until well-combined.
3. Continue mixing in flour, 1 cup at a time, up to 9 cups total. Dough should be slightly sticky but not so wet that it leaves dough stuck to your hands.
4. Turn the dough onto a floured surface and knead for 5 minutes to develop gluten. Form the dough into a compact round shape and place in an oiled bowl.

5. Turn the dough over several times to oil the surface of the dough. Cover bowl with a cloth and let rise in a warm place until double in size, about 1 hour.

6. Punch down dough and knead for another 5 minutes until smooth and elastic.

7. Grease baking sheets or line with parchment.

8. Make egg glaze by whisking together 1 egg, 1 teaspoon oil, 2 teaspoon sugar, and 1 teaspoon water in a small bowl. Refrigerate until needed.

9. Cut the dough into 4 equal parts, and cut each piece into 3 smaller pieces for a three-strand loaf. Cut into 6 if you want to do a 6-strand braid. Working on a floured surface, roll the small pieces into ropes about the thickness of your thumb and about 12 inches long. Ropes should be fatter in the middle and thinner at the ends. Pinch 3 ropes together at the top and braid them. Pinch the end together and fold under for a neat look. Place loaves onto prepared baking sheets and let rise in a warm place until doubled in size for 30–45 minutes.

10. Brush a coat of the egg glaze onto the tops of loaves and reserve remain glaze.

11. Preheat oven to 350 degrees.

12. Bake bread in preheated oven for 20 minutes, and then remove from oven and brush remaining glaze over loaves. Return to oven for final 10 minutes and bake until tops are shiny and golden brown.

13. Let cool before cutting. (If you can!)

This recipe yields a much sweeter loaf than the quick and easy challah recipe. It is well worth the extra time it takes to make! As I have been baking breads for several years now, I have developed a few tricks to make some of the steps easier. For instance, I drizzle olive oil on my surface, instead of flour, when rolling out the dough as it makes it easier to work with. I also like the way it adds a creamier taste to the loaves. I have also figured out that putting the loaves into bread pans for baking yields a nice high loaf that will work well for sandwiches. Not using bread pans yields a wider loaf as it spreads out during the rising time. Do whatever you want to make your loaves look and cut the way you want them! And when I found that putting more glaze on during the last 10 minutes of baking, well, that was what really made the loaves even more fabulous-looking!

Purim

Dinner menu

Appetizers—baba ghanoush, tahini, hummus, veggies, and pita chips for dipping
Lamb, cherry tomato, red onion kebabs
Zucchini and red bell pepper sauté
Mediterranean quinoa salad
Dessert—hamantaschen

Baba Ghanoush

1 large eggplant
1 1/2 T. tahini sauce
4 cloves garlic
/2 lemon, juiced
1/2 t. red pepper flakes (if you like!)
Salt, to taste
1 T. olive oil, to taste
1 pinch dried or fresh parsley flakes for garnish

1. Preheat oven to 400 degrees. Arrange oven racks so there is one low and one high in the oven.
2. Cut a shallow slit along the side of the eggplant and place into a baking dish.
3. Roast in preheated oven on the lower rack until the eggplant is completely shrunken and soft for about 40 minutes. Move the baking dish to the upper rack and continue baking until the skin is charred for about 5 more minutes. Let eggplant cool until cool enough to handle.
4. Peel and discard skin from eggplant. Put eggplant into a bowl; add tahini, garlic, lemon juice, red pepper flakes, and salt. Stir until all ingredients are evenly mixed. Drizzle olive oil over the Baba Ghanoush and garnish with parsley.

I love saying the name of this! I almost always use preminced garlic from a jar. That means I am never sure exactly how much minced garlic is equal to a clove of garlic! But for me, part of the fun of cooking is the guesswork! So add as much or little garlic as you like!

Tahini

1/2 c. tahini (sesame paste)
1/4 c. fresh lemon juice
1 clove garlic
1 pinch salt, to taste
2 T. warm water or as needed

1. Whisk tahini, lemon juice (add a little at a time and taste), olive oil, garlic, and salt together in a bowl until smooth and thick. Add warm water, a bit at a time if needed, whisking after each addition until desired consistency is reached. Season with salt.
2. Cover the bowl with plastic wrap and refrigerate until flavors blend for about 3 hours or more! Serve with chips or veggie sticks.

Hummus

2 cloves garlic
1 can garbanzo beans, reserve half of the liquid
4 T. lemon juice
2 T. tahini
1 t. salt
Black pepper to taste
2 T. olive oil
1 T. chopped parsley

1. In a blender, chop garlic. Put lemon juice, tahini, and salt to the blender. Put garbanzo beans into blender reserv-

ing about 1 tablespoon for garnish. Add reserved liquid, lemon juice, tahini, and salt. Blend until creamy and well-combined.

2. Transfer the mixture to a medium serving bowl. Sprinkle with pepper and pour olive oil over the top. Garnish with reserved garbanzo beans and chopped parsley.

Easy peasy! And so yummy! Serve with carrot and celery sticks and crackers of any kind. This makes a nice, light appetizer for any occasion!

Lamb, Cherry Tomato, and Red Onion Kebabs

1/4 olive oil
1 t. kosher salt
1 t. ground cinnamon
1 t. ground cumin
1/2 t. ground cardamom
1/2 t. ground coriander
Juice of 1 lime
2 lb. cubed lamb, 3/4" cubes
24 cherry or grape tomatoes
3 small red onions or 1 large, cut into chunks

1. In a large bowl, combine oil with salt, cinnamon, cumin, cardamom, coriander, and lime juice. Stir to mix well.
2. Add lamb, tomatoes, and onions. Toss to coat.
3. Marinate in the refrigerator for at least 30 minutes and up to 2 hours.
4. To make kebabs, skewer one piece of lamb followed by a tomato; add another piece of lamb followed by an onion. Repeat so that each skewer is full of lamb, 2 tomatoes, and 2 onions.
5. Broil on high for 8–10 minutes for medium doneness or 12–14 minutes for well-done. This can also be done on the grill.

Serves 6.

Tender and yummy!

Zucchini and Red Bell Pepper Sauté

3 T. extra virgin olive oil
4 medium zucchinis, use a vegetable peeler to slice into strips
4 cloves garlic, minced
4 roasted bell peppers, thinly sliced
3 t. paprika
1/2 Kosher salt

1. Heat oil in a large skillet over medium-high heat. Add zucchini strips and sauté 6–8 minutes or until slightly softened.
2. Add minced garlic and sauté 3 minutes more. Add bell pepper and sauté for 5 minutes or until warmed.
3. Stir in paprika and salt. Toss to coat.

Serves 6.

Mediterranean Quinoa Salad

Salad

1/2 c. uncooked quinoa
1 c. black olives, sliced
1 c. roasted peppers, sliced
1 c. fresh or canned corn kernels
1/2 c. red onion, diced
1/2 c. cilantro, chopped
2/3 c. feta cheese crumbles

Dressing

> 2 T. olive oil
> 2 t. red wine vinegar

> 1. Boil the quinoa in water with a pinch of salt according to package directions. Once cooked, drain and let cool.
> 2. Prepare the dressing by whisking all ingredients together.
> 3. In a medium bowl, combine quinoa and the rest of the salad ingredients and pour the dressing over. Toss and enjoy!
> 4. Serves 4.

Serves 8.

I use this recipe for Purim and Shavuot. It's great in the summertime as well because it's so easy!

Buttery Hamantaschen

3/4 c. unsalted butter, room temperature
2/3 c. sugar
1 large egg, room temperature
1 t. vanilla
1 t. orange zest
2 1/4 c. flour
1/4 t. salt
1-5 T. water (if needed)

1. Slice room temperature butter into small chunks and place in a large bowl of electric mixer.
2. Add sugar to bowl. Cream butter and sugar together for a few minutes until light and fluffy.
3. Add egg, vanilla, and orange zest to the bowl. Beat again until creamy and well-mixed.

4. Sift flour and salt into the bowl. Mix on low speed until crumbly dough forms.

5. Begin to knead dough with hands until a smooth dough ball forms. Try not to overwork the dough. If the dough is too crumbly, add water slowly, 1 teaspoon at time; use your hands to knead the liquid into the dough. Knead and add liquid until the dough is smooth and slightly tacky to the touch (not sticky) with a consistency that is good for rolling out. If the dough is too wet, add a bit more flour.

6. Form the dough into a flat disk and wrap in plastic wrap. Place in the refrigerator and chill for 3 hours to overnight.

7. Choose and make your hamantaschen filling and have it ready for assembly.

8. Preheat oven to 350 degrees.

9. Lightly flour a smooth, clean surface. Unwrap the dough disk and place on the floured surface. The dough will be very firm after chilling.

10. Using a rolling pin, roll dough out to 1/4-inch thickness. As you roll, cracks may form. Repair cracks with your fingers and continue rolling.

11. When dough reaches about 1/4-inch thickness, scrape it up with a pastry scraper; lightly re-flour the surface, and flip the dough over. Continue rolling the dough to 1/8-inch thickness. The thinner you roll, the crisper and more delicate the cookies will be!

12. Using a 3-inch cookie or biscuit cutter, cut circles out of the dough. Cut as many as you can.

13. Gather the scraps, roll out again, and cut. Repeat until there is no more dough to use! This should yield about 35 cookies unless your dough is thicker.

14. Place a teaspoon of filling into the center of each circle. Do not use too much, or it will all run and be very messy! Cover the circles you are not working with, with a damp cloth so they don't dry out.

15. Assemble hamantaschen.

To assemble

1. Grasp the left side of the circle and fold it toward the center to make a flap that covers the left third of the circle. Grasp the right side of the circle and fold it toward the center overlapping the upper part of the left side flap to create a triangular tip at the top of the circle. A small triangle of filling should still be visible in the center.

2. Grasp the bottom part of the circle and fold it upward to create a third flap and complete the triangle. When you fold this flap up, be sure to tuck the left side of this new flap underneath the left side of the triangle while letting right side of this new flap overlap the right side of the triangle. This way, each side of your triangle has a corner that folds over and a corner that folds under, thus creating a pinwheel effect.

   This method of folding pretty will help keep the cookies from opening during baking.

3. Pinch each corner of the triangle gently but firmly to secure the shape. (It should look like George Washington's hat!) If any cracks have formed, use the warmth of your fingers to smooth them out.

4. Repeat this process for all circles.

5. When all of your Hamantaschen have been filled, place them on a lightly greased baking sheet, evenly spaced.

6. Bake in preheated oven for 20–25 minutes or until cookies are cooked through and lightly golden. Depending on how thin or thick your dough is, this may take less time.

7. Cool cookies on wire racks. Cookies can be stored in a tightly sealed container or plastic bag. They also freeze well if you make them way ahead of time!

If the assembly part seems too daunting, look for an online tutorial! That's what I do! And every time I make these, I get a little better at the assembly part! Remember, practice makes permanent!

Fillings for Hamantaschen

Fillings for hamantaschen are only limited by your imagination! I use lemon curd, raspberry jam, date butter, halva, fig butter, chocolate chips, cookie butter... It is also fun for kiddos to help with the decorating! Dip in chocolate and then colored sprinkles! Mm-mmm!

Halva comes in a variety of flavors. I usually find it in the section of the store with the cream cheese. I can also find it on the shelf in the International foods section in the grocery store.

Giant Hamantaschen

2 sheets puff pastry, cut into 10×10-inch squares
6 bananas
2 T. silvan (date honey)
7 oz. dark chocolate, melted
4 eggs, plus one for egg wash
4 egg yolks (the whites can be used for meringues)
1 c. butter, melted
1/2 c. flour
1/2 c. sugar
8 squares from a chocolate bar (I like dark chocolate best!)

1. Make sure puff pastry is defrosted according to package instructions. Preheat oven to 350 degrees.
2. This recipe is for 2 giant hamantaschen. Trim two sheets of puff pastry into 10x10 inch squares. Place a bowl over each square and cut into circles.
3. Slice the peeled bananas across so that they can be straightened into a line and place them on top of the puff pastry so that they are in a triangle shape.
4. Drizzle silan on top of each banana. Roll each banana slice in puff pastry toward the center to form a triangle.

5. In a large mixing bowl, add the melted chocolate, eggs, egg yolks, butter, flour, and sugar. Mix well until there are no clumps.
6. Pour half of the mixture into each hamantaschen. Add a few squares of chocolate on top of the filling.
7. Brush the dough with egg wash and bake for 12–15 minutes until a toothpick inserted comes out clean, or still gooey and chocolatey, if you prefer a more soufflé consistency.

This recipe is much easier than the previous one if this is your first time. And it is a big hit with the family! Of course, if you don't like bananas, you are in trouble here! You could substitute chocolate sauce in place of the date honey.

Passover

Seder plate

Harroset
Maror—horseradish sauce, prepared
Parsley sprigs
Hard-boiled egg
Shank bone
Small cup of salted water
Matzo

Dinner menu

Matzo ball soup
Beef brisket
Roasted carrots with tahini glaze
Spinach-artichoke kugel
Matzo

Dessert
Passover cookies
Passover lemon loaf

Haroset

6 apples, peeled, cored, and chopped
1 c. walnuts, finely chopped
1/2 t. ground cinnamon
3 1/2 t. honey
1/3 c. sweet red wine

1. Place apples and walnuts into a large bowl.
2. Sprinkle cinnamon over apples. Stir in honey and sweet wine. Refrigerate until serving.

Makes 6–8 servings.

Matzo Ball Soup

For matzo balls

4 eggs
6 T. olive oil
1/3 c. club soda plus 2 T.
1/2 t. salt
1 1/2 c. matzo meal or more as needed
4 qt. water

For soup

1 16 oz. box chicken or vegetable stock
16 oz. water
Carrots
Celery
Onions
Salt and black pepper, to taste
Sprigs of parsley, finely chopped

1. Whisk eggs and olive oil in a bowl until combined. Stir 1/3 cup plus 2 tablespoon club soda and salt into egg mixture.
2. Mix matzo meal into wet ingredients to form workable dough. If mixture is too wet, add 1/4 cup more matzo meal. Cover and refrigerate for 30 minutes.
3. Bring water to a boil in a large pot. Wet your hands and form matzo ball dough into walnut-sized balls. Gently place matzo balls into boiling water. Reduce heat to low; cover and simmer matzo ball until tender and they float to the top of the water about 25–30 minutes.
4. In a stockpot or Dutch oven, combine stock and water.
5. Slice carrots, celery, and onions. Use as many as you like.

6. Add salt, black pepper, and parsley to taste.
7. Bring stock to a boil. Reduce heat. Add matzo balls and heat through.

Makes about 16 matzo balls.

This is one of those recipes that you can experiment with. Add as many of the vegetables as you like, but the matzo balls are the start of this show! Another way to change this up is to add some chopped, cooked spinach to some of the matzo balls. You can also add some sun-dried tomatoes to some of the matzo balls and get a very pretty combination for your soup! Serve one of each kind of matzo ball with the soup!

Beef Brisket with Prunes and Merlot

For eight servings
4 4 1/2 lb. flat-cut beef brisket, trimmed
2 T. olive oil
1 14 1/2 oz. can diced tomatoes in juice
1 c. Merlot or other dry red wine
2 lb. red onions, sliced
4 medium-sized carrots, peeled and thinly sliced
16 garlic cloves, peeled
1 1/2 c. pitted large prunes (about 8 oz.)
1 T. finely chopped thyme
1/2 c. plus 1 T. prune juice
3 T. plus 1 t. balsamic vinegar
2 T. chopped fresh Italian parsley
Salt and pepper, to taste

1. Position rack in bottom third of oven and preheat to 325 degrees F. Pat brisket dry; sprinkle all over with salt and pepper.

2. Heat oil in heavy extra-large skillet over high heat. Add brisket and cook until deep brown about 7 minutes per side.

3. Transfer brisket, fat side up, to large roasting pan. Add tomatoes with juice and wine to skillet. Remove from heat; scrape up any browned bits, and pour mixture over brisket.

4. Distribute onions, carrots, and garlic around brisket. Add prunes and thyme; drizzle with 1/2 cup prune juice and 3 tablespoons vinegar. Sprinkle with salt and pepper.

5. Place pan over 2 burners and bring to boil. Cover pan with heavy-duty foil; place in oven.

6. Braise brisket until tender for about 3 hours and 15 minutes. Uncover and cool 1 hour or so at room temperature.

   This can be made up to 2 days ahead of time and will save a lot of work on your special day! Cover with foil and chill. Bring just to simmer over 2 burners before continuing. This recipe is my go-to for both Passover and Hanukkah, why not? It's so good that I need it more than once a year!

7. Remove brisket from roasting pan, scraping off juices. Place on work surface; cut across grain into 1/4-inch thick slices. Spoon off fat from top of pan juices. Place 1 cup vegetables (no prunes) and 1 cup braising liquid from pan into processor and puree. Return puree to pan. Add remaining 1 tablespoon prune juice and 1 teaspoon vinegar to pan. Heat sauce; season with salt and pepper.

8. Overlap brisket slices in 13×9×2-inch glass baking dish. Pour sauce over brisket, separating slices to allow some sauce to flow between. *This can be done 1 day ahead! Cover; chill.*

9. Rewarm brisket, covered in 350-degree Fahrenheit oven, for 30 minutes. Sprinkle brisket parsley; serve.

Serves 8.

Brisket Overnight

3 onions
3 whole heads of garlic, sliced in half to reveal the cloves
1 whole brisket
Kosher salt
Freshly cracked black pepper
1 c. dry red wine
3 c. beef or chicken broth
1 c. crushed tomatoes (optional)

1. Preheat oven to 225 degrees.
2. Layer sliced onions and garlic in a large roasting pan or Dutch oven. Season brisket with salt and pepper.
3. Place brisket on top of onions and garlic. Pour red wine, broth, and tomatoes, if using, into pan. Cover food directly with a layer of parchment and then seal tightly with foil.
4. Roast in oven at 225 for 10 hours.
5. Carefully transfer brisket to a cutting board to cool before slicing. While brisket is cooling, strain onions and garlic from pan juices. Press onions and garlic so that all juices run out. Skim fat off of pan juices and reduce pan juices on the stovetop until it coats the back of a spoon.
6. Slice brisket across the grain and transfer back to braising pan. Store in refrigerator for up to 3 days or freeze for up to one month. Freeze juices separately.
7. Reheat brisket, covered, in a low oven at 250 degrees until hot. Serve with warmed, reduced pan juices.

Roasted Carrots with Tahini Glaze

For carrots

1 1/2 lb. carrots, peeled, trimmed, halved, and sliced into 2-inch pieces.

2 T. extra virgin olive oil
1/2 t. kosher salt, plus more to taste
1/2 t. ground cumin

For tahini glaze

1/3 c. extra virgin olive oil
1/4 c. pure tahini paste
1/4 c. freshly squeezed lemon juice
3 T. silan (date honey)
1/2 t. fine sea salt
1/4 t. cayenne pepper
2 T. water, more or less as needed

1. Preheat oven to 425 degrees. Arrange carrots on a baking sheet and drizzle with 2 tablespoons olive oil. Sprinkle with salt and cumin. Toss the carrots to coat evenly with spices.
2. Roast carrots for 20–30 minutes, turning once halfway through cooking, until the largest pieces have softened and edges are darkening.
3. While carrots are roasting, in a medium bowl whisk together 1/3 cup olive oil, 1/4 cup tahini paste, 1/4 cup lemon juice, 3 tablespoons silan, 1/2 teaspoon salt, and 1/4 teaspoon cayenne. Add water if needed until the glaze is smooth and pourable.
4. Remove roasted carrots from oven and drizzle with the tahini glaze. Use as much as you like! Toss gently to coat carrots.
5. Serve carrots warm or at room temperature.

Serves 4.

This recipe makes a lot of the glaze. It can also be used as a salad dressing or for any other roasted vegetable!

Spinach-Artichoke Kugel

5 matzos, broken into pieces
1 1/2 c. half and half
8 oz. cream cheese, softened
8 oz. sour cream
1 c. shredded cheddar cheese
1 large egg
10 oz. thawed frozen chopped spinach, drained and squeezed of excess liquid
10 oz. thawed frozen artichoke hearts
1 1/2 t. kosher salt
1 t. garlic powder
1/2 c. freshly grated Parmesan
1/4 t. crushed red pepper flakes

1. Preheat oven to 350 degrees. Mist a 9x13-inch baking dish with nonstick spray.
2. Soak matzo in half and half for about an hour or until most of the liquid is absorbed and the matzos have softened.
3. In a large bowl, combine cream cheese, sour cream, cheese, and egg.
4. Put in the spinach, artichokes, and season with salt, garlic powder, and crushed red pepper.
5. Add the softened matzo, discarding any excess liquid. Stir to combine all ingredients.
6. Pour into prepared baking dish. Bake at 350 degrees for 45 minutes or until golden around the edges and almost set in the middle.
7. Top with freshly grated Parmesan cheese.

Serves 8.

This is a savory kugel that is so creamy and wonderful! Great anytime!

Passover/Hanukkah Cookies

Sugar Cookies

1 1/2 c. butter, softened
2 c. white sugar
4 eggs
1 t. vanilla
5 c. all-purpose flour
2 t. baking powder
1 t. salt

1. In bowl of stand mixer, cream together butter and sugar until smooth. Beat in eggs and vanilla. Stir in flour, one cup at a time, baking powder, and salt. Cover and chill dough for at least an hour or overnight.
2. Preheat oven to 400 degrees. Roll out dough on floured surface 1/4–1/2 inch thick. Use Star of David and *Dreidel* cookie cutters to cut shapes. Place cookies 1 inch apart on ungreased baking sheets.
3. Bake 6–8 minutes in preheated oven. Cool completely before frosting.

For Passover, I use a cross, Star of David, cup of redemption, and Torah-shaped cookie cutters. For Hanukkah, I use Star of David—the cup of redemption cutter can be used for a Menorah—and a dreidel cutter.

Sugar Cookie Frosting

1 c. confectioners' sugar
2 t. milk
2 t. light corn syrup
1/4 t. almond extract

1. In small bowl, stir together confectioners' sugar and milk until smooth. Beat in corn syrup and almond extract until icing is smooth and glossy. If it is too thick add more corn syrup.
2. Divide into separate bowls or icing tubes with small tips. Add blue food color to one bowl, and mix a few drops of yellow and green to make brown. Leave one white for background color. Use a pastry brush to paint white icing onto stars and *dreidel*-shaped cookies.

Passover Lemon Cake

1 1/2 c. matzo cake flour
1/2 t. baking soda
1/2 t. baking powder
1/2 t. salt
3 eggs
1 c. white sugar
2 T. butter, softened
1 t. vanilla extract
1 t. lemon extract
1/3 c. lemon juice
1/2 c. vegetable oil
1 drop yellow food coloring or as desired

Frosting

1 c. powdered sugar
1–2 T milk
1/2 t. lemon extract

1. Preheat oven to 350 degrees. Grease a 9×5-inch loaf pan.
2. Whisk together the matzo flour, baking soda, baking powder, and salt in a large mixing bowl.

3. In a separate bowl, beat the eggs, white sugar, butter, vanilla, 1 teaspoon lemon extract, lemon juice, vegetable oil, and food color. Beat until smooth with an electric mixer on medium speed.
4. Pour wet ingredients into flour mixture.
5. Pour into prepared pan.
6. Bake in preheated oven until set and lightly browned for about 45 minutes. A toothpick inserted in the center of the loaf will come out clean. Cool completely before removing from pan.

Frosting

1. Place 1 cup of powdered sugar in a bowl. Stir in milk. Add more until desired consistency. Add lemon extract.
2. Spread frosting over cooled cake and allow to set.

Shavuot

Dinner menu

Falafels with pita pockets *or* Mediterranean flatbread
Goat cheese and walnut salad
Israeli couscous taboule
Mushroom cheese blintzes

Dessert
Halva cheesecake

Brunch menu

Pashtida with zucchini, corn, and tomatoes

Falafels

1 (15 oz.) can chickpeas (a.k.a. garbanzo beans), drained and mashed
3/4 c. bread crumbs
1 small, unpeeled red potato, shredded
1/4 c. diced red onion
2 cloves garlic, crushed
1 egg
1 T. olive oil
1 T. chopped, fresh cilantro
1 t. lemon juice
1 t. cumin
1/4 t. salt
1/4 t. ground black pepper
1 c. canola oil for frying

1. Combine all ingredients in a large bowl.
2. Form mixture into 2-inch round balls. Place another 1/4 cup breadcrumbs in a shallow bowl. Roll balls in the breadcrumbs to coat.
3. Heat canola oil in a saucepan over medium-high heat.
4. Fry balls in the hot oil until golden brown for about 4 minutes, turning frequently.
5. Remove balls from oil and let drain on paper towels.
6. Keep warm in oven until ready to serve.

Stuff pita with sliced cucumbers, lettuce, and sliced tomatoes. Add falafel to the pita. Drizzle with a yogurt-dill sauce or tzatziki sauce.

Easy Mediterranean Flatbread

2 t. instant yeast
1 t. granulated sugar

1 3/4 c. warm water
1/2 c. warm milk
1 T. extra-virgin olive oil
2 t. salt
5 1/2–6 c. bread flour

1. In a bowl of a stand mixer fitted with the dough hook, mix yeast, sugar, water, milk, and 2 cups of the flour until well-combined.
2. Add 1 cup flour, the salt, and oil. Continue to mix adding the flour reserving 1/2 cup. Continue mixing until soft dough forms and the dough pulls away from the sides of the bowl. The dough will be soft to the touch. Knead dough until it is soft and smooth for about 5–6 minutes.
3. Place dough in a lightly greased bowl and cover with plastic wrap. Let rise until double for about an hour.
4. Divide dough in half and half again. Cut each half into 8 pieces. Form each piece into a tight ball. Cover with a cloth or plastic wrap and let rest for about 10 minutes. This helps the dough relax, so it is easier to work with.
5. Work with one piece at a time on a floured surface. With a rolling pin, roll the dough from center outward. Turn the disc as you work. Roll the dough out to about 6 inches by 1/8 inch thick. Cover with cloth while working on next circle. Repeat until all circles are completed.
6. Heat a lightly oiled skillet to medium heat. When the skillet is hot, cook the flatbread for 2–3 minutes on the first side until it bubbles and puffs. Flip over with tongs or spatula and one on the other side until golden and spotted brown. Be careful not to overcook as it will dry out and not be bendable!
7. Transfer flatbread to a plate and cover with a towel. Repeat until all flatbreads are cooked.

These can be frozen with great results! Use anytime! To reheat, wrap in aluminum foil and heat in oven at low temperature.

Goat Cheese and Walnut Salad

Salad

    2 (5 oz.) packages mixed greens
    1 1/2 cup dried cranberries or craisins
    1 small red onion, thinly sliced
    1 (5.5 oz.) log soft fresh goat cheese, crumbled
    1 1/2 cup walnuts

1. Mix greens, cranberries, and onion in large bowl.
2. Sprinkle cheese and walnuts over salad mixture.
3. Pour dressing over salad and toss right before serving.

Dressing

    2 1/2 T. red wine vinegar
    1 T. Dijon-style mustard
    1/2 t. fresh thyme, finely chopped
    7 T. olive oil
    1/2 t. salt
    1/2 t. ground black pepper

1. Mix vinegar, mustard, and thyme in a small bowl.
2. Gradually whisk in olive oil; season with salt and pepper.
3. Toss dressing with salad immediately before serving.

I like to toast the nuts before putting them into a salad. Place nuts in a shallow baking dish and roast them in the oven at 350 degrees for 10 minutes.

Couscous Tabouleh

1 1/2 c. pearl couscous
1 c. chicken broth
3/4 c. water
1/2 c. fresh lemon juice, divided
2 1/2 t. kosher salt, divided
1/3 c. seeded cucumber cut into 1/4" pieces
2 c. cherry tomatoes cut in half
1 c. minced scallions, white and green parts
1 1/2 c. loosely packed fresh parsley, minced
1 c. loosely packed fresh mint, minced plus some mint sprigs for garnish

1. In a saucepan, combine the broth, water, 1/4 cup lemon juice, and 1 1/2 teaspoons salt. Bring to a boil and stir in the couscous. Cover and let couscous simmer for 10 minutes.
2. In a large bowl, stir together cucumber, tomatoes, scallion, olive oil, and remaining 1/4 teaspoon salt. Let mixture stand for 15 minutes. Add the couscous, parsley, and mint. Stir the salad well. Chill, covered, for an hour.
3. The salad may be made up to 2 days in advance. Keep covered and chilled. Garnish with mint sprigs before serving.

Serves 4.

Mushroom Cheese Blintzes

For crepes

This is my mother's recipe that I have used forever!

3/4 c. flour
3 eggs

1 c. milk
1 t. vanilla
Butter

1. Beat eggs in bowl of stand mixer. Gradually add flour and milk, alternating. Add vanilla and mix well to combine all ingredients.
2. Melt 1 tablespoon butter in skillet, per crepe. Pour enough batter into pan just to thinly cover the bottom of the skillet. When bottom is lightly browned, flip crepe over using a wide spatula. Brown other side.
3. Scoop crepe out of pan with spatula onto plate. Place a paper towel between each crepe so that they don't get all stuck together before filling!

Crepes can be made ahead of time and refrigerated or frozen.

Filling

3 T. butter
1 large onion, diced
2 cloves garlic, minced
2 lb. mushrooms, sliced
1/4 c. diced green pepper (optional)
3 T. flou1 C milk
1/2 t. salt
1/8 t. pepper
1/2 t. basil
1 lb. mozzarella or Monterey jack cheese, grated

1. Melt butter in a large skillet and sauté onion, garlic, mushrooms, and green pepper (if using).
2. Cook for 10–15 minutes. Add flour and stir.
3. Slowly stir in milk; add salt and pepper and basil.
4. Cook, stirring over low heat until mixture thickens.

5. Stir in cheese. When it is thick, remove from heat.
6. Assemble blintzes by filling each crepe with 1–2 table-spoons of the mushroom mixture.
7. Fry in hot oil.

Chocolate Halva Cheesecake

Crust

2 c. finely ground chocolate cookie crumbs (about 30 cookies)
4 oz. melted unsalted butter
Pinch of sea salt

1. Stir crumbs, butter, and salt together. Press into the bottom of an 8-inch springform pan. Press crumb mixture up the sides of the pan about 1 inch.
2. Refrigerate for 15 minutes.

Cheesecake filling

1 lb. cream cheese, room temperature
14 oz. can-sweetened condensed milk
2 t. vanilla extract
12 oz. marbled chocolate halvah, roughly chopped

Garnish

Additional halvah, crumble for topping

1. In a stand mixer, beat cream cheese on low, with paddle attachment, until smooth and creamy. Add sweetened condensed milk and vanilla. Beat until incorporated.
2. Mix in halvah by hand to keep from breaking it up too much.

3. Pour into the chilled crust. Refrigerate for at least 4 hours or until firm.
4. Run a spatula around the edge of the cheesecake to loosen it from the pan.
5. Remove from pan. Garnish with halvah crumbs.

If you love cheesecake, you will really love this one!

Pashtida with Zucchini, Corn, and Tomatoes

2 T. plus 1 t. olive oil
6 scallions, roughly chopped
2 zucchinis cut into 1/2" thick half-rounds
1 1/2 c. corn, frozen or canned. Fresh is better if you have 2 ears of corn!
2 1/2 c. cherry or grape tomatoes, half of them cut in half
4 eggs
3 T. flour
1/3 c. ricotta cheese
3 1/5 oz. fresh mozzarella
2 oz. cheddar cheese, grated
1 T. butter
1 handful fresh basil, chopped
Sea salt and black pepper, to taste

1. Preheat oven to 350 degrees.
2. If using fresh corn, cut off the cob with knife cutting in a downward motion.
3. Heat a medium-large skillet on high heat and add the corn kernels to the dry pan. Stir occasionally allowing them to become more bright yellow in color and a little charred. Transfer to a plate; season with a pinch of sea salt and melt half the butter over it.
4. Let the skillet cool a bit and then place it back onto medium heat. Add 1 tablespoon olive oil and then add zucchini

slices. Stir occasionally until they become slightly softened and begin to brown. Transfer to the plate with the corn and add remaining butter and a pinch of sea salt.

5. Wipe the skillet with a paper towel. On medium heat, heat 1 teaspoon olive oil and add the scallions. They should sizzle and become charred within a few minutes. Stir occasionally, then remove from pan. Add to other vegetables.

6. Add the last tablespoon of olive oil to the skillet and add tomatoes. Let them blister and soften slightly. Season with a pinch of salt and remove from heat; add to other vegetables.

7. Allow all vegetables to cool down.

8. In a mixing bowl, beat the eggs until slightly frothy. Slowly add the flour and continue to mix.

9. Add ricotta and keep mixing until all is incorporated. Season with a pinch of salt and black pepper.

10. Add the vegetables into the egg mixture reserving a little bit of each for the topping. Mix well. Shred half of the mozzarella into small pieces and add to the mixture.

11. Lightly grease an 8-inch round cake tin or pie plate with butter or olive oil. Sprinkle half of the grated cheddar cheese around the bottom and sides of tin or plate. Pour the mixture into the tin. Shred the remainder of the mozzarella over the top of the mixture and then top with remaining grated cheddar. Season again with a pinch of salt and pepper and top with the reserved vegetables and chopped basil.

12. Bake the pashtida for 30–35 minutes or until it is fluffy and cooked through.

Serves 4–6.

This is a multipurpose recipe! It's like a crustless quiche. This dish can be used for potlucks even! You could also add other seasonal vegetables and change up the cheeses. Do what tastes good to you! It sounds like there's a lot of salt and pepper going on in this recipe; use your own judgment as to how much you like. Pashtida can be served for breakfast, lunch, or dinner! Serve with a side salad for a brunch or dinner as it makes a great meal for hot summer months!

Additional Yummy Recipes, Good Anytime!

Kubaneh (Bread)

1 T. yeast
4 c. all-purpose flour
2 T. sugar
1 1/2 T. kosher salt
1 1/2 c. water
10 T. room temperature, unsalted butter, divided

1. In a large mixing bowl, combine yeast, flour, sugar, and salt.
2. Slowly add water and mix in a stand mixer using the dough hook for 6 minutes until dough is smooth, *or* knead by hand for 10 minutes until smooth.
3. Grease bowl with 1 tablespoon room temperature butter. Place dough in bowl; cover with a damp cloth or plastic wrap and let raise 1 hour or until dough doubles in size.
4. Punch dough down and divide into 8 portions. Grease a 9-inch cake pan with 1 tablespoon butter.
5. On a very lightly floured surface, start forming each portion of dough into the kubaneh (circular) shape by taking a bit of butter in your hand and smoothing out the dough into a thin circle.
6. Spread some more butter over the circle of dough spreading the dough as thin as you can. A few rips may occur, but that's okay!
7. Roll dough up like a jellyroll. Then roll it into a snail-like shape and place in greased pan. Repeat for all eight portions of the dough. (Should look like cinnamon rolls!)
8. Cover with damp kitchen cloth or plastic wrap and let rise for 30 minutes.
9. Preheat oven to 350 degrees.
10. Bake for 30 minutes, uncovered.

Your hand will be a buttery mess! But this is really worth the effort it is so good! This Yemenite pull-apart bread is usually eaten on Shabbat for breakfast. But it is great anytime, any day!

Chocolate Babka Challah

Use either of the challah recipes. While the dough is rising, make the chocolate filling:

4 oz. dark chocolate, finely chopped
2 T. olive oil
1/4 t. salt
3 T. sugar
1/2 t. ground cinnamon
1/8 t. ground ginger
1/8 t. ground nutmeg
3 T. olive oil
1/4 c. cocoa
1/4 c. sugar

1. Melt the chocolate with the oil in a saucepan over low heat. Add sugar, salt, and spices to the pan and stir to combine. Refrigerate to cool until needed.
2. On a floured surface, using a rolling pin, roll the risen dough out to an 18×10-inch rectangle, long side close to you. Brush the 3 tablespoons of olive oil over the dough.
3. Sprinkle the cocoa over the greased dough. Top with sugar and mix with your hands to combine.
4. Top with the melted spiced chocolate mixture and use a spatula to swirl it out over the dough.
5. Starting with the long side farthest from you, roll dough into a tight log, pinching firmly along the seam to seal. Coil the log to form a round challah and place on a baking sheet, lined with parchment, to rise for about 40 minutes.
6. Make the crumble.

For the crumble

    1 c. all-purpose flour
    1/2 c. firmly packed brown sugar
    1 t. salt
    1/2 t. ground cinnamon
    1 stick unsalted butter, softened but cool

1. Combine all ingredients except for the butter in a medium bowl and give a quick stir to combine, making sure to break up any lumps of brown sugar.
2. Add the butter and use your fingertips to mix everything together until crumbs form. Set aside until needed.
3. Place rack in middle position in the oven and preheat to 275 degrees. Bruch the top of the challah with egg wash. Sprinkle with crumble.
4. Bake until the top is a deep golden brown for about 40–50 minutes.
5. Transfer challah to wire rack and cool to room temperature.

This recipe is killer! It is good for a dessert served with fruit and whipped cream! It is almost like a dense cake! But it is also wonderful, warmed, for breakfast!

Easy Tahini Cookies

2/3 c. Tahini
1 t. vanilla
1 egg
2/3 c. sugar
Pinch of salt
1/2 c. all-purpose flour

1. Preheat oven to 350 degrees.
2. Add all ingredients in a bowl except the flour and mix.

3. Add flour and mix until the dough looks crumbly.
4. Using your hands, take a small piece of dough and shape it into a small ball. Place on cookie sheet.
5. Place ball on parchment-lined cookie sheet. Press each ball in the middle with your thumb and place an almond in the space. Or you can use a fork to flatten each ball in a crisscross pattern.
6. Bake for 10 minutes. All done!

I have also made these with gluten-free flour and the recipe works great! You can't tell the difference! These cookies are addicting! They are great with coffee or tea anytime!

Jerusalem Bagels

On my first trip to Israel (when I was young and single), I would buy a large bagel in the Old City for lunch. It was very filling, cheap, and I just loved them! When I went again, a couple of years ago, I rediscovered them and was not disappointed! I was so excited to find this recipe after returning home.

Bagel

3 T. white sugar
2 1/4 t. active dry yeast
1 t. salt
3 T. olive oil
1 1/4 c. warm water
3 c. all-purpose flour

Topping

Cold water
Sesame seeds
Poppy seeds

Mixed seeds
Olive oil

1. Combine sugar, yeast, salt, olive oil, and warm water in a large mixing bowl. Stir.
2. Gradually add flour until dough begins to form.
3. Move dough onto a floured flat surface and knead for 5 minutes until no lumps are left in the dough.
4. Place dough back into mixing bowl (oil it a bit so the dough doesn't stick).
5. Cover with a cloth and let rise 45 minutes.
6. Preheat oven to 400 degrees.
7. Dump dough onto flat surface and separate into tennis-ball-sized shapes.
8. Using two fingers, make a hole in the middle of the circle and then stretch it out into a large circle.
9. Put some cold water into a shallow pan. Dip the circles into the cold water and then place on a baking sheet.
10. Sprinkle seeds of your choice over the tops of the bagels. Let rest for 10 minutes.
11. Bake in preheated oven for 15–20 minutes until lightly golden brown.
12. Brush generously with olive oil as soon as you take them out of the oven.

These are incredibly good! They do not last very long in my house! Mm-hmm!

Matzo Granola

3 sheets matzo, crushed into tiny pieces
1/3 c. pecans, chopped
1/3 c. almonds, chopped
1/4 c. unsweetened shredded coconut
3/4 t. cinnamon
1/8 t. nutmeg
1/8 t. salt
1/4 c. honey
1/4 c. olive oil
1 t. vanilla extract
Craisins
Dates
Raisins

1. Preheat oven to 325 degrees. Line a baking sheet with parchment paper.
2. In a large bowl, combine the matzo, nuts, coconut, and spices. Set aside.
3. Melt the honey in the microwave or over low heat on the stove. Stir in olive oil and vanilla extract.
4. Stir the honey mixture into the matzo mixture and toss to fully coat.
5. Spread the mixture into an even layer on the prepared baking sheet.
6. Bake for 15 minutes then remove from oven and stir.
7. Bake for an additional 10 minutes or until golden brown.
8. Take out of the oven and let cool completely.
9. Add craisin, chopped dates, or raisins to your desired taste. Stir.
10. Pour into container with airtight lid.

This is one of those recipes that you can do so many variations on! I use the gluten-free matzo because I think it is crunchier. I also like both craisins and dates mixed in. This good for snacking, but I also eat it with plain yogurt and cranberry applesauce.

Liturgies for the Feasts

In each of these liturgies, I have provided some notes that I hope will add clarification and increase understanding. These notes are delineated by an asterisk (*) and are not necessarily to be included in the readings. However, you may decide it helps you and your family and guests gain more clarity and encourages a stronger sense of worship. Depending on who is sitting at my table will depend on how much explanation is needed. Create some space especially for questions if there are young ones present! It doesn't need to be "formal."

Rosh Hashanah/Yom Kippur

* The celebration of the Jewish New Year is the anniversary of the creation of Adam and Eve, a day of judgment, and coronation of God as King.
* Blowing the *shofar* is important to this day. Typically, three types of blasts are used: a long, sob-like blow; three short wail-like blows; nine piercing short staccato bursts.

The blowing of the *shofar* represents the trumpet blast that is sounded at a king's coronation. It also serves as a call to repentance as well as a call for the people to gather.

Lighting of the Candles

*   Leviticus 23 tells of the Lord's commands to celebrate certain festivals and how the children of Israel are to do so. These festivals are referred to as "holy convocations." *Rosh Hashanah*, or New Year, is celebrated on Tishri 1 (in the Jewish calendar). This is not the biblical date but the civic date that has been determined by the rabbis of the tenth or eleventh century to be the day that God created the world.

As the candles are lit, say this prayer: Blessed are You, Lord our God, King of the universe, who has sanctified us with his commandments and has commanded us to light the candle of Shabbat and of the Day of Remembrance.

> LEADER. Blessed are you, O God, King of the universe! You have blessed us through this past year and we are thankful for your graciousness to us.
>
> ALL. God of all glory, on this first day of creation, bring light out of darkness. On this first day, you began your new creation raising Jesus Christ out of the darkness of death.
>
> LEADER. On this day, grant that we, the people you created, by water and the Spirit may be joined with all your world in praising you for your great glory.
>
> ALL. We confess our sins to you and ask that you make us like a tree planted by the water that we might bring forth firstfruits of good living in due season.
>
> LEADER. Forgive our past offenses and sanctify us now, and direct all that we should be in the future. Thank you for your gracious gift of forgiveness through the sacrificial gift of your

only Son, Jesus Christ our *Lord*, in whose name we pray, *amen* (taken from *The Worship Sourcebook*).

Sing together "This Is My Father's World."
Words by Maltbie D. Babcock, traditional English melody. Adapted by Franklin L. Sheppard.

Call to Repentance

READER 1.

> Is there any other God like You, who forgives evil and passes over the transgressions done by Yours who remain? He does not hold onto His anger forever because He delights in showing love and kindness. He will take pity on us again, will tread our wrongdoing underfoot. He will cast all our sins down to the bottom of the sea. (Micah 7:18–19)

* These verses allude to the mercy of God. We ask for his mercy even as we ask for his forgiveness for wrongdoing.
* Leviticus 16 tells how God commanded Moses and Aaron to make a sacrifice on behalf of all the people for their sins. Aaron was to bring two male goats to the Tabernacle: one was for the sacrifice and the other was to be sent into the wilderness as a scapegoat. Aaron was to place both hands on the head of the live goat and confess all the sins of the people and then send it away into the wilderness. This was done so that the people could be cleansed from their sin, and God would receive their worship.
* This is the picture that God gave to represent how he would later send his Son into the world to be the final sacrifice or scapegoat for all sins.

READER 2.

> For God expressed His love for the world in this way: He gave His only Son so that whoever believes in Him will not face everlasting destruction, but will have everlasting life. (John 3:16)

READER 3.

> You see, all have sinned, and all their futile attempts to reach God in His glory fail (Romans 3:23).

*   This is why Jesus came to, once and for all, save us from our sins. He became the only sacrifice that is now needed. All we need to do is confess our sins, and he will be faithful to forgive us!

ALL.

> Look on me with a heart of mercy, O God, According to Your generous love. According to Your great compassion, wipe out every consequence of my shameful crimes. Thoroughly wash me, inside and out, of all my crooked deeds. Cleanse me from my sins. For I am fully aware of all I have done wrong, and my guilt is there, staring me in the face. It was against You, only You, that I sinned, for I have done what You say is wrong, right before Your eyes. So when You speak, You are in the right. When You judge, Your judgments are pure and true. (Psalm 51:1–4)

Sing together "Create In Me A Clean Heart."

Words and music by Keith Green, 1984 for the shepherd music (ascap) admin at capitolcmgpublishing.com

READER 4.

> But think about this: while we were wasting our lives in sin, God revealed His powerful love to us in a tangible display—the Anointed One died for us. As a result, the blood of Jesus has made us right with God now, and certainly he will rescue us from God's wrath in the future. (Romans 5:8–9)

> LEADER. While it is true that we have sinned, it is a greater truth that we are forgiven through God's love in Jesus Christ. To all who humbly seek the mercy of God, I say in Jesus Christ, your sin is forgiven.
> ALL. Thanks be to God!
> LEADER. Hear these comforting words: If you repent and believe in God's redeeming mercy, your sins are forgiven. Trust in God's promises and begin anew your life with God and people in the name of Jesus Christ.

Sing together "You Are My King / Amazing Love."
Words and music by Billy J. Foote CCLI Song # 2456623, 1996 worshiptogether.com songs

Blessing for the bread

> Blessed are you, Lord our God, King of the universe, who brings forth bread from the earth.

Blessing for the meal (dinner), blow the shofar

* The rabbis believe that Messiah will come on Rosh Hashanah or Yom Kippur when the shofar is blown. For true believers in Jesus as Messiah, we do not know the day or the hour when he will come again. But we are to prepare ourselves and be ready for his second coming.

LEADER.

Now the Lord is not slow about enacting His promise—slow is how some people want to characterize it—no, He is not slow but patient and merciful to you, not wanting anyone to be destroyed, but wanting everyone to turn away from following his own path and to turn toward God's. The day of the Lord will come unexpectedly like a thief in the night; and on that day, the sky will vanish with a roar, the elements will melt with intense heat, and the earth and all the works done on it will be seen as they truly are. (2 Peter 3:9–10)

Let us proclaim together the mystery of our faith:

ALL. Christ has died. Christ is risen. Christ will come again!

Sukkot

*   As you enter the *sukkah*, remember that the children of Israel wandered in the desert for forty years. We are also strangers wandering through this world looking forward to the blessed hope when Messiah will establish a new kingdom!

READER.

> See, the home of God is with His people. He will live among them; They will be His people, And God Himself will be with them. (Revelation 21:3)

Wave the *lulav* and offer these blessings:

1.   Blessed are you, Lord our God, King of the universe, who has sanctified us with his commandments and commanded us regarding the *lulav.*
2.   Blessed are you, Lord our God, King of the universe, who has granted us life, sustained us, and enabled us to reach this occasion.

*   On these days, holiday candle lighting in the Sukkah precedes the night meals. Before lighting the candles say:
3.   Blessed are you, Lord our God, King of the universe, who has sanctified us with his commandments and has commanded us to kindle the light of the festival day.
4.   Blessed are you, Lord our God, King of the universe, who has granted us life, sustained us, and enabled us to reach this occasion.

A Brief Liturgy for Advent at Home

* Assign readers for each of the four weeks. Either keep the readers the same each week, or mix them up! Sing Christmas carols that go along with each week.

Week 1, first Sunday, hope

> READER 1. Jesus said, "I am the Light of the world; the one who follows me will not walk in darkness but have the light of life" (John 8:12). We light this first candle as a sign of the coming light of Christ (light the first purple candle).
>
> READER 2. This first candle reminds us of the light of hope that the prophets had in their expectation of a Messiah who would bring peace and love to the world.
>
> READER 3. The people who had been living in darkness have seen a great light. The light of life has shined on those who dwelt in the shadowy darkness of death (Isaiah 9:1–2).
>
> ALL. Come, Lord Jesus, our light and life. Until that day, let us walk in the light of the Lord.

Sing "O Come, O Come, Emmanuel."

Week 2, second Sunday, peace

> READER 1. In anticipation, we gather. With expectation, we wait. We gather to watch for the coming of the good news into our world and into our lives. We wait to see the fullness of God's vision. *Light the first purple candle.*
>
> READER 2. (in prayer) O God, open the doors to our hearts that this year, we may have room

for the birth of Jesus. O God, as we marvel over all that you are doing, overwhelm us with so much wonder that words of praise spring forth from our lips! In this time of waiting, let true worship begin in our hearts. Let our praises rise up to the heavens!

READER 3. Let our celebrations spread new hope over a tired world! Let us gather together all our dreams and lives to worship our God! Amen.

READER 4. The first candle reminds us of the light of hope of the prophets. *Light the first purple candle.*

LEADER. The second candle reminds us of the messenger that came to tell the people that to be God's people; they must be obedient to God. *Light the second purple candle.*

READER 5. I will lead the blind by a road they do not know; by the paths they have not known, I will guide them. I will turn the darkness before them into light, the rough places into level ground. These are the things I will do, and I will not forsake them (from Isaiah 42 and 45).

ALL. Come, Lord Jesus, our light and life. Until that day, let us walk in the light of the Lord.

Sing "O Little Town of Bethlehem."

Week 3, third Sunday, joy

LEADER. We gather in preparation for good news is about to be proclaimed. We gather in expectation for joy is about to explode in our midst. We gather in celebration for we are those people who have said yes to the manger, yes to love made flesh, yes to the one incarnate for others, yes to the wholeness of God. With preparation and in expectation, let us celebrate!

READER 1. The first candle reminds us of the light of hope of the prophets. *Light the first purple candle.*

READER 2. The second candle reminds us of the messenger that came to tell the people that to be God's people, they must be obedient to God. *Light the second purple candle.*

READER 3. The third candle reminds us of the great light and joy which surrounded the shepherds at the announcement of Jesus's birth. *Light the pink joy candle.*

READER 4. The messenger said, "Don't be afraid! Listen! I bring good news, news of great joy, news that will affect all people everywhere. Today, in the city of David, a Liberator has been born for you! He is the promised Anointed One, the Supreme Authority! You will know you have found him when you see a baby, wrapped in a blanket, lying in a feeding trough."

READER 5. At that moment, the first heavenly messenger was joined by thousands of other messengers—a vast heavenly choir. They praised God saying, "To the highest heights of the universe, glory to God! And on earth, peace among all people who bring pleasure to God!"

ALL. Come, Lord Jesus, our light and life. Until that day, let us walk in the light of the Lord.

Sing "The First Noel."

Week 4, fourth Sunday, love

> READER 1. The first candle reminds us of the light of hope of the prophets. *Light the first purple candle.*
>
> READER 2. The second candle reminds us of the messenger that came to tell the people that to be God's people, they must be obedient to God. *Light the second purple candle.*
>
> READER 3. The third candle reminds us of the great light and joy which surrounded the shepherds at the announcement of Jesus's birth. *Light the pink* joy *candle.*
>
> LEADER. The fourth candle reminds us of the great love that God had for us in giving his Son, Jesus, to die on the cross for us. *Light the last purple candle.*
>
> READER 4. For God so loved the world that he gave his one and only Son that whoever believes on him shall not perish but have life eternal. For God did not send his Son into the world to condemn the world, but to save the world through him (John 3:16–17).
>
> READER 5. But if we walk in the light, as he is in the light, we have fellowship with one another, and the blood of Jesus, his Son, purifies us from all sin (1 John 1:7).
>
> ALL. Come, Lord Jesus, our light and life. Until that day, let us walk in the light of the Lord.

Sing "O Come, All Ye Faithful."

Christmas Eve/Christmas Morning—The Christ Candle

READER 1. The first candle reminds us of the light of hope of the prophets. *Light the first purple candle.*

READER 2. The second candle reminds us of the messenger that came to tell the people that to be God's people, they must be obedient to God. *Light the second purple candle.*

READER 3. The third candle reminds us of the great light and joy which surrounded the shepherds at the announcement of Jesus's birth. *Light the pink* joy *candle.*

READER 4. The fourth candle reminds us of the great love that God had for us in giving his Son, Jesus, to die on the cross for us. *Light the last purple candle.*

READER 5. *Light the center white candle.* Jesus said, "I am the light of the world, he who follows Me will not walk in darkness, but will have the light of life."

READER 6. We light this candle as a sign of the coming Christ. We light the center candle to remind us that Jesus will come again to reign, and we will live with him forever.

ALL. Come, Lord Jesus, our light and life. Until that day, let us walk in the light of the Lord.

Sing "Joy to the World!"

Hanukkah

* For each night, light the *shammash*, and use it to light the appropriate number of candles and read the corresponding scripture.

Light the Shammash—The Highest Candle

Isaiah 60:19 says, "You won't need the sun to brighten the day or the moon and lamps to give you light. The Eternal One will be all the light you ever need. Your God will provide your glory, brilliance for all time."

The sun and moon are natural lights. We use them to see and make our way around in the natural world. That is what God intended. But God has another kind of light for us. He showed us a picture of this light in the holy place of the tabernacle (later the temple). The holy place was completely closed off to daylight by thick coverings. But inside it was a wonderful light called the menorah—the seven-branched oil lamp that God himself designed. The light from this menorah lit up the Holy Place of God just like his Holy Spirit lights up the inside of believers now. Remember, we are called the temple of God in the New Testament. As we read God's Word and hide it inside us, the Holy Spirit of God will give us revelation as to what this Word means to us. You have a menorah inside of you—God's revelation light operating in your life by the power of the Holy Spirit. As you seek this light and walk by it, it will keep you from danger and sin. And you yourself will begin to glow with the light of God as you become like him through obedience. God will be your glory (through the Holy Spirit) as the scripture above says. As you dedicate yourself to the Word of God and seek the illuminating revelation of the Holy Spirit, you will shine like a light in this world.

Lighting the Second Candle

Because, although you were once the personification of darkness, you are now light in the Lord. So act like children of the light. For the fruit of the light is all that is good, right and true. Make it your aim to learn what pleases the Lord. Don't get involved with the fruitless works of darkness: instead, expose them to the light of God. (Ephesians 5:8–11)

* It is recommended that a *Hanukkah* menorah be placed in the window of your home during *Hanukkah*. It is thought in Judaism that those who have strayed from their Jewish faith might see its light and be drawn back to God. And so it is with the menorah within us. As we live out the life of God, it is visible to others. Praise be to God!

After the blessings are recited, liturgy read, and candles are lit, you can sing traditional *Hanukkah* songs. These are easily accessed online on a variety of sites.

Lighting the Third Candle

But if someone responds to and obeys His word, then God's love has truly taken root and filled him. This is how we know we are in an intimate relationship with Him: anyone who says, "I live in intimacy with Him," should walk the path Jesus walked. My loved ones, in one sense, I am writing a new command for you. I am only reminding you of the old command. It's a word you already know, a word that has existed from the beginning. However, in another sense, I am writing a new command for you. The new command is the truth that he lived; and now you are living it, to, because the darkness is fading and the true light is already shining among you. (1 John 2:5–8)

Jesus was the perfect light who came down from heaven to serve us. He didn't have to come; he wanted to. He came to serve us in many ways, but most of all, he was the "suffering servant" who was "obedient even unto death" so he could purchase our pardon from sin with his blood and then purify us with his own righteousness. He came down even as the servant candle "comes down" from its perch to bend over and serve the other candles. And in this serving, he lights us up with his own light!

Lighting the Fourth Candle

"On another occasion, Jesus spoke to the crowds again. 'I Am the light that shines through the cosmos; if you walk with Me, you will thrive in the nourishing light that gives life and will not know darkness'" (John 8:12).

How good to know that we don't have to walk in darkness. Jesus lights up the spiritual darkness that we once walked in. That is cause for celebration! And Hanukkah is a time for celebrating. Traditionally, Jewish people sing and dance as part of their celebration. Find some traditional Jewish songs and learn the hora (a traditional Israeli folk dance), or make up your own circle dance!

Lighting the Fifth Candle

(John 10:22–42) It was winter and time for the Festival of Dedication (Hanukkah). While in Jerusalem, Jesus was walking through the temple in an area known as Solomon's porch, and Jews gathered around Him.

> JEWS. How long are you going to keep us guessing? If you are God's anointed, the liberating King, announce it clearly.
>
> JESUS. I have told you, and you do not believe. The works I am doing in my Father's name tell the truth about me. You do not listen; you lack faith because you are not my sheep. My sheep respond as they hear my voice; I know them intimately, and they follow me. I give them a life that is unceasing, and death will not have the last word. Nothing or no one can steal them from my hand. My Father has given the flock to me, and he is superior to all beings and things. No one is powerful enough to snatch the flock from my Father's hand. The Father and I are one.
>
> NARRATOR. The Jews gathered stones to execute Jesus right then and there.
>
> JESUS. I have performed many beautiful works before you in the name of the Father. Which of these can be judged as an offense that merits my execution?
>
> JEWS. You are not condemned for performing miracles. We demand your life because you are a man, yet you claim to be God. This is blasphemy!
>
> JESUS. You know what is written in the Scriptures. Doesn't it read, "I said, you are gods?" If the Scriptures called your ancestors (mere mortals) gods to whom the word of God came—and the Scriptures cannot be set aside—what should you call One who is unique, sanctified

by and sent from the Father into the world? I have said, "I am God's Son." How can you call that blasphemy? By all means, do not believe in me if I am not doing the things of the Father. But examine my actions, and you will see that my work is the work of the Father. Regardless of whether you believe in me, believe the miracles. Then you will know that the Father is in me, and I am in the Father.

NARRATOR. Once again, some of the Jews tried to capture him, but he slipped away, eluding their grasp. Jesus crossed the Jordan River and returned to the place where John was ritually cleansing the people through baptism in the early days. He lingered in the area, and scores of people gathered around him.

CROWDS. John never performed any miracles, but every word he spoke about this man has come to pass. It is all true!

NARRATOR. In that place, many believed in him.

* See how Jesus wanted the people to believe him! He performed many miracles to point them to his divine and messianic identity. The message of Hanukkah is that God is actively involved in the affairs of his people. He is a God of miracles, not just some esoteric ideals! He broke through human history and continues to do so into our lives today!

Lighting the Sixth Candle

Your word is a lamp for my steps; it lights the path before me. When Your words are unveiled, light shines forth; they bring understanding to the simple. (Psalm 119:105, 130)

> For their direction is a lamp; their instruc-
> tion will light your path, and their discipline will
> correct your missteps, sending you down the
> right path of life. (Proverbs 6:23)

These verses show us how important the Word of God is to our everyday walk of life. We can use the Word of God just as we would a flashlight or lantern to guide us in the darkness. First of all, it shows us the right path instead of all the paths that the world and other people are trying to get us to walk in. And then it will even show us our particular steps to walk in on that path. The Word will be our guide so that we do not take a false path or a false step in that path. And it can help us return if we do get out of the path of life.

Also, these verses show us that without the Word, we don't really have true understanding. God's Word shows us things that we would not have understood otherwise, and so we are able to act and speak the way God would want us to and not according to our own understanding.

God's ways are not our ways, and we need his light to penetrate us and lead us. We talked about this somewhat on our first night. As we prayerfully read the Word of God, our Holy Spirit menorah will bring revelation light to us to give us understanding and show us our path. God is so good that he doesn't leave us without this light and then even provides the power (by the Holy Spirit within us) to do these things which are not easy for us because part of our soul has not yet learned to submit to godly ways.

A side note, in Biblical times, when walking at night, people would tie small oil lamps to their shoes! See? This was how the path would be lit as they walked!

Lighting the Seventh Candle

> The eye is the lamp of the body. You draw
> light into your body through your eyes, and light
> shines out to the world through your eyes. So

if you eye is well and shows you what is true,
then your whole body will be filled with light.
(Matthew 6:22–23)

You can read many interpretations of this verse, but let us look at a "Jewish roots" interpretation. In the Jewish culture, having a "good eye" meant that you were a generous person. In other words, you just love being a person who gives. Having a "bad eye," on the other hand, meant that you were a stingy, greedy person who only gave grudgingly what he felt like he "had to give."

It is interesting that in the *Hanukkah* traditions, there is one associated with money. No one can say for sure where it came from. Some say that, because Torah study was forbidden in the days of wicked King Antiochus, there came to be a tradition of giving money so that children would have the means to go to a school where they could study Torah (meaning the Scriptures in our understanding).

Jesus equates having a generous spirit with being full of light. Let us always remember to be generous with our money and our time and our talent whenever and wherever Jesus directs us to be.

Lighting the Eighth Candle

Light is among you, but very soon it will flicker out. Walk as you have the light, and then the darkness will not surround you. Those who walk in darkness don't know where they are going. While the light is with you, believe in the light; and you will be reborn as sons and daughters of the light. (John 12:35–36)

Jesus Christ is the light of the world. One of the Rabbis said Light is the name of the Messiah; as it is written in Daniel 2:22 that *light* dwells with him. God is light, and Christ is the image of the invisible God—God of gods, Light of lights. He was expected to be a light to enlighten the Gentiles (Luke 2:32), and so is the light of the world and not of the Jewish church only. The visible light of the world is the sun, and Christ is the Son of righteousness. One sun enlightens the whole world, and so does one Christ. Christ, in calling himself the light, expresses the following:

1. What he is in himself—most excellent and glorious.
2. What he is to the world—the fountain of light, enlightening every person. What a dungeon would the world be without the sun!

"So would it be without Christ by whom
light came into the world" (John 3:19).

Pray, O God, seal into our hearts and bring to our remembrance as we need them—the things that we have learned and heard from you in these eight days of light. May we, as God's temple, be rededicated to you in this season. Amen.

The Story of Purim—The Feast of Lots
Long Version
(Based on the Book of Esther from *The Voice* Bible)

Cast of characters:

Narrator
King Ahasuerus (a.k.a. Xerxes)
Mordecai
Hadassah (a.k.a. Esther)
Queen Vashti
Haman
Memucan
Harbonah, a servant
Zaresh—Haman's wife
Various officials and servants

NARRATOR. Our story opens during a time in the land of Persia after Darius the Great had died. His son, Ahasuerus, was king. He was not a God-fearing man like his father had been. He was foolish and weak. The capital of the Persian Empire had been Babylon. But that city was destroyed, so Shushan became the capital. It was even more magnificent than Babylon! King Ahasuerus lived there in great splendor. His mighty empire stretched from India in the Far East to Ethiopia, south of Egypt, in the west. It was as big as the United States. In the third year of his reign, the King invited all the princes and nobles of his kingdom to a wonderful feast in the capital city of Shushan. The party lasted for six months! At the end of that time, all the people of the city were invited to a great feast. Men only attended the feast as women were not allowed in a place where men gathered. While the king entertained the men, the queen, Vashti, gave a feast for the women inside the palace. The feast lasted a week.

KING AHASUERUS. (*drunkenly*) Bring Queen Vashti to my party! Tell her to put on her royal crown *and to wear her finest clothes*. I want to show off her beauty in front of my distinguished guests.

QUEEN VASHTI. I will do no such thing!

KING AHASUERUS. Queen Vashti has blatantly defied me and refused the order I gave her through my assistants! Tell me, good men, what do the laws of this land suggest should be done to a queen who has disobeyed her king?

MEMUCAN, *before the king and nobles*. Your queen has wronged you, my king. She has also offended every noble of the land and all the people who reside in your provinces. Something must be done! If we don't act quickly, every woman in this kingdom will hear about Queen Vashti's disrespect for you, and they will follow her example in dishonoring their husbands. I can hear the women now talking among each other: "Why should we listen to our husbands when Queen Vashti doesn't come when King Ahasuerus calls for her?" This day, the noble women of Persia and Media who hear what the queen has done will respond in kind to your nobles, and there will be chaos all across the land. But, my king, don't worry; I have an idea! With your permission, of course, I recommend that a decree be issued among the Persians and the Medes—a law that cannot be repealed that forbids Vashti from ever being allowed in your presence again. In fact, I would further suggest that you give her position to another woman—someone who is more honorable than she is. As your subjects hear about your decree in the far reaches of your kingdom, all the women will stop and give their husbands the honor they deserve, those of royal blood as well as the commoners. Oh, this is a great idea!

KING AHASUERUS. That is a brilliant idea! I say we make Memucan's counsel into law!

SERVANT. O, King, someone should find beautiful young women who are old enough to be married for you. We suggest you appoint officers in every province of Persia to round up every eligible woman and add her to your harem in the citadel of Shushan. Hegai, who is in charge of the harem, will see to it that all of the women are properly prepared and receive all the needed cosmetics. Then, whichever young woman delights you the most will reign as queen in Vashti's place.

KING AHASUERUS. I like the idea! Go, execute the plan! Look for the most beautiful girls in all the land!

MORDECAI. Esther! Look at this! *(He shows her the decree.)* The king is seeking a new queen!

OFFICIAL, *to Esther.* You! Girl! Come with me to the palace!

The official presents Esther to the king. Ahasuerus places the crown on her head.

> SERVANTS. *(Whispering to each other.)* We must kill the king...the king has got to go!
> *Mordecai overhears the plot. He runs to tell Esther.*
> MORDECAI, to Esther. Esther, you must get a message to the king to tell him that there are people plotting to kill him!
> OFFICIAL, *to the king.* Your Majesty, a plot has been uncovered.
> OFFICIAL, *to the scribe.* Make a record of what has transpired and have the plotters hanged.
> AHASUERUS, *to Haman.* You are my favorite prince. I give you many honors so that all will know you are my favorite. All will show you respect by bowing to you.

Haman walks through a crowd, and all bow low as he passes by except for Mordecai.

> OFFICIALS. *(Looking at Mordecai.)* Why are you disobeying the king's command?
> OFFICIALS TO HAMAN. Look, this Jew refuses to bow and obey the king's command.
> HAMAN, *to himself.* Who does this Mordecai think he is? Is he more important than me? Am I not the king's favorite? How can I make him bow to me? I must come up with a plan! But not just have him to have him hanged. No, all of his people must die as well! I must find the luckiest day to carry out my plan. I will cast lots until I find the luckiest day. *(Haman rolls dice several times.)*

HAMAN, *to the king*. O, King, may you live forever! There is a group of people scattered abroad among the nations in all of the provinces of your kingdom. Their laws are different from the laws of all other people. They do not keep the king's laws; therefore, it is not for the king's profit to let them live. If it pleases the king, let it be written that they be destroyed. I will pay ten thousand talents (dollars) into the king's treasury so that the king will not lose any taxes by having them killed.

KING AHASUERUS, *to Haman*. The money is yours and the people are yours also to do with as you wish.

OFFICIAL, *in a big voice*. The king's decree! On the thirteenth day of the twelfth month, you are to kill all the Jews both young and old, little children, and women.

MORDECAI, *in a loud wailing voice*. How can this be! O, God of our fathers, how can we be saved now?

ESTHER, *to servant*. Go to Mordecai at once. Find out why he is wailing, and report back to me everything that he says.

MORDECAI, *to servant*. Tell the queen Haman has pledged lots of money to place into the royal treasury in exchange for the destruction of the Jews. Look, here is a copy of the order for mass murder of the Jews—the same order issued in the city of Shushan. Show it to Esther. Tell her everything I have told you. Convince her to go before her king and plead for his mercy not only for her life but also for the lives of her people.

ESTHER. How am I supposed to see the king? It's known throughout the land, from the greatest of the king's officials to the common folk who live in the provinces, that any person who approaches the king in the inner chamber without being invited is sentenced to death. That's the law! There's only one exception, and that's if the king were to hold out the gold scepter to that person and spare his or her life. It's been thirty days since the king last called for me!

MORDECAI, *to servant.* Tell Esther, "Don't be fooled. Just because you are living inside the king's palace doesn't mean that you out of all of the Jews will escape the carnage. You must go before your king. If you stay silent during this time, deliverance for the Jews will come from somewhere, but you, my child, and all of your father's family will die. And who knows? Perhaps you have been made queen for such a time as this."

ESTHER. Tell Mordecai, "In preparation for my audience with the king, do this: gather together all the Jews in Shushan, and fast and pray for me. Intercede for me. For three days and nights, abstain from all food and drink. My maids and I will join you in this time. And after the three days, I will go in to the king and plead my people's case even though it means breaking the law. And if I die, then I die!"

KING AHASUERUS. What is it, Queen Esther? What is your request? I'll give you anything— even half of my kingdom. All you need to do is ask.

QUEEN ESTHER. If it would please you, my king, I'd like for you and Haman to come today to a banquet I have made in your honor.

KING AHASUERUS. *(Looking at his servants.)* Go and find Haman this instant so we can do as Esther desires.

KING AHASUERUS. Now, my queen, what is your request? I promise that half of my kingdom is not too much to ask! Don't be afraid to ask for whatever you want.

QUEEN ESTHER. I do want something. My request is, If I have found favor before you, and if you truly desire to grant my request, would you and Haman join me again tomorrow for another banquet I will prepare? Then I will answer your question.

HAMAN, *to his cronies.* And that's not all! Queen Esther invited me today to have dinner with her and the king. Just the three of us! And guess what? She's invited me again tomorrow. What do you think about that? But I must be honest, seeing that Jew, Mordecai, as I pass through the gate makes it difficult to celebrate any of my good fortune.

ZERESH. You should make a wood pole seventy-five feet high! Tomorrow morning, have the king sentence Mordecai to be executed on it. Then you'll be able to have a good time at the banquet with the king.

HAMAN. That's a brilliant idea!

Officials reading the chronicles as the king paces the floor.

KING AHASUERUS, *to his servants.* Did Mordecai receive any recognition for discovering the plot to kill me? Was he honored in any way?

SERVANTS. He received no recognition for this.

KING AHASUERUS. Is anyone out in the court now?

SERVANTS. Haman is here waiting in the court to see you.

KING AHASUERUS. Allow him to come in.

Haman enters.

KING AHASUERUS. Haman, I want to ask you something. What do you believe is the proper manner in which to honor a man who has pleased me?

HAMAN. (*Puffs out his chest.*) If you desire to honor a man, I believe you should do this: First, have your servants bring one of the robes you have worn and one of the horses you have ridden that has worn the royal crown on its head. Then you should give the robe and horse to one of your most noble officials. Have him robe the man whom you want to honor and then lead the man on horseback throughout the center of the city. It should be announced that this is what happens for the man whom the king wants to honor.

KING AHASUERUS. Your idea is perfect, Haman. I want you to go and do this immediately. Take one of my robes and one of my horses and do exactly what you have suggested to Mordecai—the Jewish man who sits at my gate. Do everything you have said, and don't leave out one single detail. Not one!

Haman looks mortified. He puts his robe and crown on Mordecai.

HAMAN. *(Shouting to all.)* This is what happens
for the man whom the king desires to honor!

ZERESH, *to Haman.* You must be very careful with
how you handle Mordecai! If he really is a Jew,
a descendant of the nation that defeated your
ancestors, then you won't be able to beat him.
In fact, you will most certainly be humiliated!
Look, you've already begun to bow to him.

NARRATOR. In the middle of their conversation, a
few of the king's servants arrived at Haman's
house and rushed him off to have dinner with
Esther and the king.

*King Ahasuerus and Haman came to dine with Queen Esther, and
while they were drinking wine, the king posed his question once again.*

KING AHASUERUS. What is your request, Queen
Esther? I'm willing to give you anything you
want. Just make your request. Even if it's half
the kingdom you desire, I will make it happen!

QUEEN ESTHER. If you love me, my king, and if it
pleases you, spare my life. That's all I'm asking
for—that my people and I be spared. That is
my wish. There are some, my king, who wish
to rid your kingdom of us. For my people and
I have been sold, marked for destruction and
massacre. Now if the plan were simply to sell
our men and women into slavery, I would
have kept my mouth shut because that would
not have been important enough to disturb
you, my king.

KING AHASUERUS. Who has targeted your people? Where is this man who dares to do this?

QUEEN ESTHER. *(Pointing to Haman.)* The man responsible for these actions is wicked Haman. He is vile and an enemy to my people.

The king exits. Haman throws himself toward Esther and begs for her to spare his life.
The king returns.

KING AHASUERUS. Haman, will you even violate my queen right here in the palace where I can see you?

HARBONAH. Look! Haman has prepared a seventy-five-foot pole for execution in his own courtyard. He was hoping to use it to hang Mordecai—the man who spoke up and saved the king.

KING AHASUERUS. Well, hang him on it!

NARRATOR. So they took Haman and killed him and displayed him on the pole he had made ready for Mordecai. And King Ahasuerus' anger subsided.

On the same day, King Ahasuerus gave Queen Esther all the household of Haman—the enemy of the Jews. Then Mordecai was brought before King Ahasuerus, for Queen Esther had told the king how they were related. The king took off his signet ring (the one he had taken back from Haman) and gave it to Mordecai. Then Esther put Mordecai in charge of Haman's entire household.

Esther came before the king once more. This time she fell at his feet, wept, and begged the king to do something to stop the evil plan that Haman had brought upon the Jews. The king, as before, extended his golden scepter to Queen Esther, and she stood to her feet before him.

QUEEN ESTHER. If it pleases the king, and if I am in his favor, and if the king believes it is the right and just thing to do, let there be an official decree written that will cancel out the order that Haman had written to rid all the king's provinces of the Jews. For I can't bear to see this catastrophe brought against my people; how can I live another day if I witness the destruction of my kindred?

KING AHASUERUS, *to Queen Esther and Mordecai the Jew.* Look, I have given you, Queen Esther, Haman's household because of his vengeful actions against your people. That is also why he hangs on the pole he had made for Mordecai. I have done all I can do; the rest is your responsibility because no order that has been written in the name of the king and sealed with the king's signet ring can be overturned. So you must write a new order to the Jews to remedy the situation; it too must be written in the king's name and sealed with the king's signet ring.

Although Haman is dead, the order to kill all the Jews in the Persian Empire is very much alive. Once the king has signed an order, it cannot be reversed. Such kings never reverse themselves; it is too risky. So a new order must be written and sent to the far reaches of the empire, and Mordecai, the Jew, is just the person to do it. Now that he has been elevated to the supreme position where he has use of the king's signet ring, he can exercise royal power.

NARRATOR. So the royal secretaries were summoned together on the twenty-third day of the third month (the month of Sivan). The king's new orders were written down exactly the way Mordecai dictated them, and they were written to the Jews, the rulers, the governors, and the nobles of the 127 provinces stretching from India to Ethiopia. The orders were written down in every script and every language spoken in the provinces, including the Jewish script and the Jewish language. Mordecai wrote in the name of King Ahasuerus and sealed it with his signet ring. Then, these orders were dispatched to the provinces by couriers who rode on the finely bred horses sired by the royal stud. The king's new orders gave the Jews in every city the right to gather together, to protect themselves, and to kill or destroy any army of any nation or province (including their women and children) who might attack them. The orders also gave the Jews the right to take over the assets of their enemies. These new orders were set to go into effect on the thirteenth day of the twelfth month (the month of Adar). This was the same day Haman had determined by casting lots to kill the Jews. An official copy of the king's order was to be issued to every province and read publicly to all nationalities so that the Jews would be ready to protect themselves against their enemies. The couriers were quickly dispatched by order of the king, and they left the capital riding on royal steeds. Then the decree was publicly proclaimed in the citadel of Shushan.

Mordecai went out from the king's presence wearing blue and white royal robes, a large gold crown, and a fine linen and purple cape. When the people of the city of Shushan saw this, they exploded into joy. For the Jews, it was a time of celebration. Darkness had turned to light, sadness to joy, shame to honor. In every city and province, wherever the king's law and orders were received, there was happiness and joy among the Jews. They feasted; they danced, and they celebrated. People from other nations living among the Jews professed to be Jews because they were afraid of the Jews' sudden political power in Persia.

KING AHASUERUS. The Jews have killed five hundred men in the capital of Shushan alone and also the ten sons of Haman. How many must they have killed in the other provinces? Now, do you want anything more? Whatever you ask will be given to you. So tell me, what further do you need? I will grant whatever that is.

QUEEN ESTHER. If it pleases the king, allow the Jews in Shushan one more day to exact justice on their enemies according to your decree. And let Haman's ten sons be displayed on the pole.

NARRATOR. The king honored Queen Esther's wishes. An order was issued in the city of Shushan, and the dead bodies of the ten sons of Haman were displayed. So on the fourteenth day of the month of Adar, the Jews killed three hundred men in Shushan. But they didn't touch any of their assets.

In short, Haman, the enemy of all Jews everywhere, had schemed against the Jews to destroy them. He did so by casting the lot (also known as the "pur"). That was the beginning of the plan to annihilate them and bring about their ruin. But King Ahasuerus learned about his evil plot and wrote an order that

Haman should receive the very punishment that he himself wanted the Jewish people to suffer. So the king directed that Haman and all ten of his sons be killed and displayed on the pole. So this is why they call these days of feasting "Purim" from the word "pur," which means "lot." It is also because Mordecai's correspondence had instructed Jews across the empire to remember what they had seen and what had happened to them. So the Jews made it their custom that every family and every descendant and every future convert would observe these two days each year in the way that Mordecai asked. This explains why these days were remembered and celebrated by all Jews in all places and at all times; the days of Purim would never be forgotten, and their celebration would never stop.

Queen Esther utilized her full authority as queen to affirm a second letter by Mordecai, the Jew, regarding Purim. So Mordecai sent letters to all the Jews in the 127 provinces of King Ahasuerus' kingdom. His letter included encouraging words of peace and truth, and it was his hope to establish these days of Purim permanently on the calendar as days of mourning and fasting for future generations as it was for them. Esther's authority affirmed the tradition of Purim, and it was written down in the official records.

Purim—Feast of Lots
Short Game Version
Rules for the Game

1. Decide who will go first. Person 1 puts on a costume and begins the story. When person 1 stops, another person quickly puts on another costume and continues.
2. While person 2 is telling the next part of the story, another person can put on costumes and props and be ready to jump in to continue the story.
3. Repeat until the story has been told to everyone's satisfaction!

Feel free to make up your own rules for play!

To make the play even more fun, create some costumes using facemasks and crowns, party noisemakers (groggers), props such as a sword and shield, a scroll, goblets, crowns, etc.

Synopsis

The story is set in Shushan, Persia. The king decides to hold a fabulous feast and invites noblemen from all over the world to attend. Women were not allowed to eat with the men. They had their own party in a different part of the palace. Mordecai is a Jew who works for the king. He discovers a plot to kill the king. Haman also works for the king. Haman and Mordecai do not get along. Esther is Mordecai's cousin. She wins a beauty contest and becomes the queen. Haman plots to kill all the Jews. Mordecai finds this out and tells Esther. Esther must do something to save her people.

King. The king decides to bring the queen to his party… She declines; the king throws a tantrum. The queen is banished. An idea for her replacement comes from Memucan, the king's aid. A beauty pageant is held.

Mordecai. A plot is hatching to kill the king. Mordecai tells Esther that she has to do something about it. She tells the king. The plotters are hanged, recorded in the chronicles.

Haman. One of the kings favored noblemen. All the people would bow down when he passed except Mordecai. Haman hatches a plot to kill Mordecai and not only to kill Mordecai but also all the Jews. Haman asks the king to make a law, which the king grants.

Mordecai. He discovers the plot and tells Esther that she has got to do something or all the Jews will be destroyed.

Esther. She tells Mordecai she will handle it. She invites the king and Haman to a banquet. She tells Mordecai to have all the Jews fast and pray for her.

King. He tells Esther he will grant her anything she wishes.

Esther. She gets cold feet and asks them to come to another banquet the next day.

Haman. He brags to all his friends how the queen favors him. He continues to stew over his hatred for Mordecai and the Jews. He makes a plan to have Mordecai hanged.

King. He can't sleep one night and calls in a servant to read to him from the chronicles. He asks the servant if anything was done to reward Mordecai for uncovering the plot to kill the king. He decides to ask Haman what should be done to show honor to someone.

Haman. He thinks that it is he that the king wants to honor, so he comes up with putting on the honoree the king's robe and crown; letting him ride the king's horse; parade through the city.

King. He tells Haman to do this to Mordecai.

Haman. He leads Mordecai through the city shouting, "This is what happens for the man whom the king desires to honor!" Then some servants came and rushed Human off to the second banquet.

King. He again asks Esther what it is she wants.

Esther. She tells the king about the plot to destroy her people.

King. He asks, Who has done this evil thing?

Esther. She points to Haman. He is found out! The king is furious and leaves the room.

Haman. He begs the queen to spare his life.

King. He returns and sees Haman almost touching the queen! A servant tells the king that Haman has already made gallows for Mordecai, so the king says to hang Haman on it.

Esther. She pleads with the king to call off the mass murder of her people.

King. He honors the queen's wish and figures out a way to allow the Jews to defend themselves when the day comes.

Mordecai. After the Jews defended themselves against the Persians, Mordecai wrote letters to all the Jews in the kingdom. His letter included words of encouragement, peace, and truth and to establish the feast of Purim permanently as days of mourning and fasting for future generations as it was for themselves.

Blessing

Blessed are you, Lord our God, King of the universe, who wages our battles, defends our rights, avenges the wrong done to us, punishes our oppressors in our behalf, and brings retribution upon all our mortal enemies. Blessed are you, Lord, who exacts payment on behalf of His people Israel from all their oppressors; God who delivers. Amen.

Passover Haggadah
"The Telling"

> The Israelites had lived in the land of Egypt for a total of 430 years. On the last day of their 430th year, all the forces belonging to the Eternal left the land of Egypt. This was the night when the Eternal kept watch over His people and brought them safely out of the land of Egypt; now this night is to be kept by His people, to be celebrated by all of the people of Israel throughout all generations. (Exodus 12:40–41)

LEADER. It is required of each of us to imagine that we too were slaves in Egypt and have been delivered from our slavery.

The Passover, or *Pesach*, is a celebration of the Israelites deliverance from slavery and their Exodus from Egypt. It is the story of God's intervention in the lives of his chosen people. Orchestrated by the God of our fathers—Abraham, Isaac, and Jacob—we see a word picture of God's eventual plan of salvation through one final sacrifice for sin.

We will read our way through the story of the Exodus, following the *Haggadah's* order of service, reciting the ancient blessings and following rituals that have been recited and acted out by Jews for centuries.

We will eat specific foods designed to help us identify with the pain of slavery experienced by our ancestors.

We will read of supernatural deliverance provided by the Great I Am.

As believers in Jesus the Messiah, *Yeshua Ha Mashiach*, we will also see how the story can be made to apply to our own journey out of slavery to sin, to redemption from our sin, through our faith in the final sacrificial lamb, Jesus the Messiah.

Washing of Hands

Washing hands before beginning a meal is an ancient custom in the Middle East and especially of the Jewish people.

In Jewish tradition, it is not done to wash away dirt. Rather, it is meant to symbolically cleanse one from defilement, having perhaps touched something that would render one "unclean."

In ancient times, a pitcher of water, along with a basin and towels, was passed around to guests. In the time of Jesus, this included washing both hands and feet and was customarily done by a servant. Presumably, unless the hands-and-feet-washing ritual was completed, the guest could not enter the host's home.

The washing of hands is traditionally performed as step number 4 of the *Seder*. The Talmud asks, "Why do we wash our hands at this point in the *Seder*?" It answers by explaining that it is an unexpected activity, thus prompting children to ask questions.

READER.

> *Jesus, knowing that He had come from God and was going away to God, stood up from dinner and removed His outer garments. He then wrapped His Himself in a towel, poured water in a basin, and began to wash the feet of the disciples, drying them with His towel.* (John 13:4)

SIMON PETER (*as Jesus approaches*): Lord, are you going to wash my feet?

JESUS: Peter, you don't realize what I am doing, but you will understand later.

PETER: You will not wash my feet, now or ever!

JESUS: If I don't wash you, you will have nothing to do with me.

PETER: Then wash me, but don't stop with my feet. Cleanse my hands and head as well.

Did Jesus perform the feet washing at that point so that he could explain that the disciples needed cleansing from him? Indeed, unless we allow ourselves to be cleansed by the Master, we are not clean, we are defiled. Unless we are clean, we cannot be part of the body of Christ followers or enter into the Father's house. Jesus humbled himself, as a servant would, to provide the cleansing we need, allowing us to have a relationship with God and to enter our Heavenly Father's house.

All perform the hand washing ritual.

The Blessing of the Festival Candles

LEADER. We begin our Passover Seder by lighting candles and reciting these two ancient blessings:

Blessed are you, Lord our God, King of the universe, who has sanctified us with His commandments and has commanded us to kindle the light of the Festival Day.

Blessed are you, Lord our God, King of the universe, who has kept us alive and sustained us and let us reach this time.

As Christ followers, we add this blessing:

ALL. Blessed are you, Lord our God, King of the universe, who has sanctified us through faith in the Messiah, the light of the world, and in his name, we kindle the Passover lights.

The Exodus story is told through the use of four cups of wine, representing the four "I wills," as recorded in Exodus 6:6–7.

LEADER. I am the Lord...

ALL.

> *I will* bring you out from under the yoke of the Egyptians.
> *I will* free you from being slaves to them.
> *I will* redeem you with an outstretched arm and with mighty acts of judgment.
> *I will* take you as my own people, and I will be your God. Then you will know that I am the Lord your God, who brought you out from under the yoke of the Egyptians.

The First Cup
The *Kiddush* Prayer—Blessing over the Cup of Wine

> LEADER. I will bring you out from under the burdens of the Egyptians.

This is God's promise, the first "I will," promising that he would provide relief to the Hebrews by bringing them out from under the harsh labor imposed upon them by the Egyptians.

All raise your cup of wine and recite the following blessing but do not drink.

> ALL. Blessed are you, Lord our God, King of the universe, Creator of the fruit of the vine.
> LEADER. Blessed are you, O Lord our God, ruler of the world, who chose us out of all the people and selected us over all the nations and made us holy through his commandments. Lovingly, O Lord our God, you have given us festival days for joy, this feast of Passover [on the] anniversary of our freedom, a holy assembly honoring our departure from Egypt,

for you have chosen us and made us holier than other people [and caused us to inherit the Shabbat] and your holy festivals did you give us lovingly and kindly with happiness and joy.

ALL. Blessed are you, O Lord, who made holy the *Shabbat*, the people of Israel and the festivals.

LEADER. Jesus said, *"It has been My deep desire to eat this Passover meal with you before My suffering begins. Know this: I will not eat another Passover meal until its meaning is fulfilled in the kingdom of God."* He took a cup of wine and gave thanks for. Then He said, *"Take this; share it among yourselves. Know this: I will not drink another sip of wine until the kingdom of God has arrived in fullness"* (Luke 22:15–18).

All drink the first cup of wine (or take a sip from your own glass).

The *Karpas*—Dipping of the Parsley

READER.

Joseph died, and so did all of his brothers. It was not long before that entire generation was gone. But the people of Israel were prolific; they had children easily, and their numbers increased rapidly. As their numbers grew, so did their strength. Eventually, they filled the land.

One day, a new king came to power and ruled over Egypt, but this new king had no knowledge of Joseph. He said, "Look! There are more Israelites than ever before, and they are growing more powerful than we are. We need to be careful in our dealings with them. Otherwise, they may grow even greater in number, and in a time of war, join forces with our enemies, fight against us, and then leave the land."

So the Egyptian authorities enslaved the Israelites and appointed cruel slave drivers over them to oppress them with hard, backbreaking labor. (Exod. 1:6–11)

LEADER. We will take our parsley and dip it into the salt water. The salt water reminds us of the tears shed in slavery and oppression. The parsley represents the hyssop that was used to place the blood on the doorposts and lintel, thereby saving the firstborn from death.

As Christ followers, we are reminded of the shed blood of Jesus that will save us from God's judgement. It allows, like the guest with the clean hands and feet, to enter into God's house.

All take the parsley and dip it into the salt water and recite the following blessing:

ALL. Blessed are you, Lord our God, King of the universe, Creator of the fruits of the earth.

Eat the parsley.

Breaking of the Middle *Matzo* and the *Afikomen*

LEADER. This decorative pouch contains three pieces of *matzo*, each in its own pocket within the pouch and is called a "unity." Jewish tradition tells us that the reason why there are three pieces of *matzo* used at Passover is because

one loaf of bread is normally used at a daily
meal, and two loaves of bread are used on the
Sabbath. (The two loaves are a reminder of
the double portion of manna, which fell on
Friday, before *Shabbat*, while Israel wandered
in the wilderness.)

Traditionally, these three pieces of matzo are called Cohen,
Levi, and Israel, representing the priests, the Levites, and the Jewish
people. The middle *matzo* is broken and a portion of it is placed in
linen and hidden away. This is called the *Afikomen*, which means
"that which comes after" or "dessert."

*At this point, if there are young children present, they should cover
their eyes while the host hides the wrapped Afikomen somewhere in the
house. The hidden piece will be recovered and eaten at the end of the
meal.*

LEADER. The *Mishnah*, Jewish oral tradition, says
that the *Afikomen* has become the substitute
for the lamb, the original Passover sacrifice.
The lamb was the last thing eaten at a Passover
Seder during the eras of the Tabernacle and
the First and Second temples.

Let's remember that lambs for Passover had to be perfect and
without any defect to be acceptable for sacrifice. After the destruction of the Temple and the discontinuation of the Passover lamb sacrifices, the Jews substituted the lamb with *matzo*.

It is thought that the broken *matzo* tradition began after the
destruction of the Temple in Jerusalem (in AD 70) and was instituted
by the Nazarenes. The Nazarenes were the sect within Judaism com-
prised of those who believed that Jesus was the promised Messiah.
The Nazarenes sect was acceptable within the Jewish community
then. There were some areas of disagreement, much like the Pharisees

and Sadducees (or today's Protestant denominations!). They were still all accepted as Jews.

Looking through our believer's lens, it seems clear that the "unity" pouch represents the Trinity: God the Father, Jesus the Son, and the Holy Spirit. The broken *matzo* piece, the *Afikomen*, comes back at the end of the Seder. The broken *matzo* symbolized Jesus's broken and sacrificial body, which rose from the dead. We believe that Jesus was the final sacrifice needed to pay for the sins of all people. Not just the Jewish nation, but all people.

The Eternal One said to Moses, *"Go visit Pharaoh and give him My message: The Eternal says to you, 'Release My people, so that they may serve Me'"* (Exod. 8:1).

The Story of the Exodus

LEADER. Often, when one tells the Passover story, it begins in Exodus 2. But it really began earlier, with the great famine in Genesis 47, which eventually brought Jakob/Israel and his entire family to Egypt.

Exodus 1 lists Israel and his seventy family members that moved to Egypt. They were not uninvited; they came at the invitation of Pharaoh!

Exodus 2 continues generations later. Moses was born and ended up being raised in Pharaoh's household. He was given the finest education. He was expelled from Egypt and became a shepherd in Midian. It was there that God called to Moses from the burning bush. I Am had heard the cry of his children, the slaves in Egypt. He declared that he would redeem them. He gave Moses instruction for how to affect the redemption plan.

Moses was a reluctant servant of God to begin with. But he was God's choice. We see clearly that his life, from infancy, was orchestrated by God. Perhaps Pharaoh's court would never have let him approach if not for Moses' previous position as a prince. Would

Moses have had the ability to organize and lead the Israelites for forty years without his splendid Egyptian education? Or his experience as a shepherd of stupid sheep?

> All things work together for good to them
> that love the Lord, and all called according to his
> purpose. (Rom. 8:28)

The next chapters in Exodus tell us of the first nine plagues. Only then, do we get to Exodus 12 and the tenth plague, where God instructed Moses on the killing of the lamb and the spreading of the blood to preserve the firstborn.

God gave specific instruction in the selecting of, roasting, and eating of the lamb. Here is where God also instituted the seven-day Feast of Unleavened Bread. It was also here that God gave the following instruction: "Therefore shall you observe this day throughout your generations".

READER.

> *Pharoah sent for Moses and Aaron before the night was over. He said to them: "Get up and get out. Leave my people right now—you and all the rest of the Israelites. Go and worship this god of yours, the Eternal One, just as you have said. Take your flocks and your herds as well with you—just as you said—and go! But bless me on your way out!*
>
> *The Egyptians frantically urged the people of Israel to hurry and leave their land. They said; "If you do not leave soon, we will all be dead."*
>
> *So, the Israelites hurried. They took their bread dough before any yeast had been added, packed up their kneading bowls, wrapped them in some of their clothing, and carried them on their shoulders.*

The people of Israel also did what Moses had told them to do; they asked the Egyptians for items made of silver and gold, and they asked for extra clothing as well.

The Eternal caused the Egyptians to have a favorable attitude toward His people, so the Egyptians fulfilled these requests and gave the people what they asked for. This is how the Israelites stripped the Egyptians of their valued possessions. (Exod. 12:31–36)

The unity matzo is lifted for the blessing. All recite the following blessing:

> ALL: This is the bread of affliction, which our ancestors ate in the land of Egypt; let those who are hungry enter and eat it, and all who are in distress come and celebrate the Passover. At present, we celebrate it here, but next year, we hope to celebrate it in the land of Israel. This year, we are servants here, but next year, we hope to be free in the land of Israel.

The Cup of Plagues—I Will Deliver You from Slavery

All fill the second cup of wine (or sip from your previous cup at the appropriate time).

> LEADER. I will free you from being slaves [to the Egyptians]. This is God's promise, the second "I will," promising that he would bring the Hebrews out from under the cruel rule of the Egyptians. He would not just relieve their oppression; he would *free* them!

Question: The youngest child asks, "Why is this night different from all other nights?"

Answer: We were slaves to Pharaoh in Egypt, and the Lord redeemed us with a mighty hand. If the Holy and Blessed One had not taken our fathers out of Egypt, then we, our children, and our grandchildren too would be Pharaoh's slaves in Egypt. This is why, even though we might be wise and learned and experienced, though we might know the Torah well, it is our duty to tell the story of the outgoing from Egypt. And the more one tells of the outgoing from Egypt, the more praiseworthy he is.

The Four Questions (Asked by the Youngest Person at the Table)

Question 1: On all other nights we eat either leavened or unleavened bread, why on this night do we eat only *matzo*, which is unleavened bread?"

Answer: This night is different from other nights because we remember our slavery in Egypt, that we were without hope, and we celebrate our freedom, which the Lord orchestrated for us. Don't forget, it is required of each of us to imagine that we too were slaves in Egypt. And that we too were delivered from our slavery.

We eat *matzo* on this night because our fathers had no time to bake proper bread with yeast. The sun baked the flat bread as the people rushed out of Egypt to begin their journey to freedom.

Question 2: On all other nights we eat vegetables and herbs of all kinds, why on this night do we eat only bitter herbs?

Answer: We eat the bitter herbs to remind us that our fathers were slaves in Egypt and their lives were bitter.

Question 3: On all other nights we never think of dipping herbs in water or in anything else, why on this night do we dip the parsley in salt water and the bitter herbs in *haroset*?

Answer: We dip the parsley in salt water to remember the tears of our enslaved fathers. We eat the *haroset* to remind us of the mortar that our fathers had to mix as cement for the bricks. We eat the bitter herbs with the sweet *haroset* to remind us that even in midst of affliction, there is always the sweetness of hope.

Question 4: On all other nights we eat either sitting upright or reclining, why on this night do we all recline?

Answer: We recline at the table because reclining was a sign of a freeman long ago, and since our forefathers were freed on this night, we recline.

> LEADER. How do these questions and answers apply to us as Christ followers? We know that our unredeemed selves are without hope. The Bible uses yeast as a symbol for sin. The Israelites rushed to leave Egypt, leaving out the leaven in their bread. We should rush to leave behind our sinful behavior once we have been given freedom.
>
> Our freedom is not a physical one. Rather, it is freedom from the judgement and eternal punishment, which we all deserve.
>
> "Those who don't know history are doomed to repeat it." We have heard this often quoted. We *should* be remembering our prior enslavement to sin, not to continually be punishing ourselves but to never forget our salvation.

After listing several sins, the apostle Paul wrote, "*Some of you used to live in these ways, but you are different now; you have been washed clean, set apart, restored, and set on the right path in the name of the Lord Jesus, the Anointed, by the Spirit of our living God*" (1 Cor. 6:11). And a few verses later, "*God will make a way to escape*" (1 Cor. 10:13).

Four times in the Torah, we are told to teach our children about the Exodus from Egypt. The sages concluded that meant that there were four types of children, and that each child would ask a different question about the Exodus.

The wise child. This child wants to know the meaning of all the rules. This child is proud to be Jewish and interested in sharing experiences that are important to Jews.

The wicked child. In today's vernacular, a child would ask, "Why and what does any of this *Seder* have to do with me?" This is a child's way of saying that they have no feeling or allegiance to the Jewish people. One interpretation is that, in Egypt, this child would not have followed the instruction to save their firstborn, and thus would have died in Egypt, a slave forever.

The simple child. What is the night all about? With clear explanation and teaching, this child will come to love Passover and appreciate its message of redemption.

The child who does not even think to ask. This child does just that, not ask questions. Parents must take the initiative to bring this child into the fold. All children should be told the story, beginning not just with Israel coming to Egypt to escape the famine, but beginning with Abram, the Patriarch, whom God called. Explain why Abraham was rewarded for his friendship with God and his obedience to God.

The Exodus Story Continues...

> LEADER. And the Egyptians treated us harshly by enslaving us and giving us heavy work to perform. We cried to the Lord, and he heard our cry, saw our oppression and our sorrow. The Lord brought us forth with a strong hand and an outstretched arm, with great terror and with ten great signs and wonders. God said, "I will pass through the land of Egypt; I will smite every firstborn."

I, Myself,
and not an angel.
and not a Seraph.
I, Myself, and not a messenger.
I, the Eternal, I am He, and none other.
On all the gods of Egypt, I will execute judgement.

God inflicted ten plagues upon the Egyptians before Pharaoh would finally let the people go free. As we read each plague, we dip our finger in the wine and let it drip three times onto our plates.

The Ten Plagues (Blood, Frogs, Gnats, Flies, Animal Disease, Boils, Hail, Locust, Darkness, Death of the Firstborn)

Dayenu: We would have been satisfied.

LEADER. If God had merely rescued us from Egypt…
ALL.

Dayenu.
Punished the Egyptians… *Dayenu.*
Destroyed their gods… *Dayenu.*
Slain their firstborn… *Dayenu.*
Given us their property… *Dayenu.*
Split the sea for us… *Dayenu.*
Brought us through on dry ground… *Dayenu.*
Drowned our oppressors… *Dayenu.*
Supplied us in the desert for forty years… *Dayenu.*
Fed us with manna… *Dayenu.*
Given us Shabbat… *Dayenu.*
Brought us to Mount Sinai… *Dayenu.*
Given us Torah… *Dayenu.*
Brought us to the land of Israel… *Dayenu.*
Built us the Temple… *Dayenu.*

LEADER: We would have been satisfied! How much more are we indebted for the manifold bounties which the Eternal hath bestowed upon us! He brought us forth from Egypt, executed judgement upon the Egyptians and their gods, slew their firstborn, gave us their wealth, divided the sea for us, caused us to pass through its midst on dry land, drowned our adversaries in the sea, supplied us with everything during forty years, fed us with manna, gave us *Shabbat*, lead us to Mount Sinai, gave us Torah, brought us to the land of Israel, and built the holy temple for us to atone for our iniquities.

READER: As Christ followers, to this, we add:

If he had merely sent the perfect lamb to be our Passover sacrifice, Jesus, His son, but had not invited us to be adopted into his family... *Dayenu.*

If he had merely adopted us into his family, but not given us eternity with him... *Dayenu.*

We could go on. How much more are we indebted for the manifold bounties which the Eternal has bestowed upon us!

Jesus said, *"I came to give life with joy and abundance"* (John 10:10). So let's add a couple more.

If Jesus had merely come to give us life... *Dayenu.*

But he did more. He gave us abundant life... *Dayenu!*

May we be truly grateful!

Eating of the Passover Foods (Pesach, Matzo, Maror, Korech)

Pesach: The Lamb, Passover Offering

Question: Why was it eaten during the days of the Temple?

Answer: Because the Eternal, blessed be he, passed over the houses of our ancestors in Egypt, as it is said, "Ye shall say, it is a sacrifice of the Passover unto the Lord, who passed over the houses of the children of Israel in Egypt, when he smote Egyptians, and spared our houses, and the people bowed themselves and worshipped."

Matzo: The Bread

Question: This unleavened bread that we eat, what does it mean?

Answer: Unleavened bread is eaten because the bread did not have time to rise when the Israelites rushed out of Egypt.

The plate of matzo is lifted, and All recite:

> Blessed are You Lord our God, King of the universe, who sanctified us with His commandments and commanded us to eat the unleavened bread.

All eat a piece of matzo.

Maror: The Tears

Question: This bitter herb that we eat, what is the reason for it?

Answer: It is eaten because the Egyptians embittered the lives of our ancestors in Egypt. All their labor was imposed upon them rigorously.

Now dip a piece of matzo into the bitter herbs and recite:

ALL. Blessed are you Lord our God, King of the universe, who sanctified us with his commandments and commanded us concerning the eating of unleavened bread.

Korech: The Hope

But those who trust in the Eternal One will regain their strength. They will soar on wings as eagles. They will run—never winded, never weary. They will walk—never tired, never faint. (Isa. 40:31)

LEADER. Let us take two pieces of *matzo* and make a sandwich using the *haroset*, dipping it into the bitter herbs. As we eat the sandwich, we recall how our fathers were able to endure the bitterness of slavery because of the sweetness of hope.

Notice that we have not touched the hard-boiled egg. It is a symbol of the Passover offering, the lamb. Lamb is no longer eaten for Passover since the destruction of the Temple, when all sacrifices for sin ceased.

ALL. Blessed are you, Lord our God, King of the universe, who sanctified us with his commandments and commanded us concerning the eating of bitter herbs.
LEADER.

There will come a time when your children ask you, "What is this thing we are doing?" You will say, "With a strong hand the Eternal led us out of Egypt and freed us from lives of slavery." (Exod. 13:14–15)

This is why we tell the story over and over!

For God expressed His love for the world in this way: He gave His only Son so that whoever believes in Him will not face everlasting destruction, but will have everlasting life. (John 3:16)

Remember the wicked son who asked, "What has that to do with me?" If we fail to want to become part of the family of God, by accepting the sacrifice of God's Son, then we are lost. If we do, then we too can say, "It is because of that which the Lord did for *me*, when I came out of bondage [of sin]."

The Hallel: Psalms of Praise

Typically, the entire passage from Psalm 113–118 is recited.

ALL.

Praise the Eternal! All of you who call yourselves the children of the Eternal, come and praise His name. Lift Him high to the high place in hearts. At this moment, and for all moments yet to come, may the Eternal's name ascend in the hearts of His people. At every time and in every place—from the moment the sun rises to the moment the sun sets— may the name off the Eternal be high in the hearts of His people. (Psalm 113:1–3)

All raise their cup of wine but do not drink from the cup.

> LEADER. We are, therefore, duty bound to thank, praise, laud, glorify, exalt, honor, bless, extol, and adore our God, who performed all these wonders for our fathers and for us. For he took us out of slavery into freedom; out of misery into happiness; turned mourning into holiday; darkness into daylight; and brought us out of bondage into redemption.
>
> ALL. Hallelujah! Then shall we, with a new hymn, give thanks to you, O Lord our God, for our deliverance and for the redemption of our souls. Blessed are you, O Eternal, who has redeemed Israel.
>
> LEADER. Remember, all believers are grafted into the tree, therefore "Israel" applies to more than just Jewish people!

Lift the second cup of wine and together recite:

> Blessed are you, Lord our God, King of the universe, Creator of the fruit of the vine.

All drink from the second cup and finally, it is time to eat our meal!

> LEADER: Now that we have eaten our meal, let us all give thanks and offer praise to the Lord.
>
> ALL: Praised are you, Adoni our God, Ruler of the universe, who in goodness, mercy, and kindness gives food to the world. Blessed is our God, whose food we have eaten and by whose goodness we live. Praised are you, Adoni our God, who provides food for all life. Blessed

be your name forever in the mouth of every living thing. Praise be the Creator of life!

The Cup of Redemption

All fill the third cup of wine.

> LEADER. I will redeem you with an outstretched arm and with mighty acts of judgment. This is God's promise, the third "I will," promising that he would not only bring the Hebrews out from under the cruel rule of the Egyptians and make them free but would do so in a grand and strong fashion.

We are going to return to the *Afikomen.* Remember that after the Temple's destruction, the *matzo* came to represent the sacrifice of the lamb. We've eaten our meal. The tradition is that final food eaten is the *matzo* in the linen wrapper.

Does the *Afikomen* ritual sound somewhat like the death and resurrection of Jesus? Luke says that Jesus was wrapped in linen for burial. (Thankfully, we don't have to wait three days for our Passover *matzo* to be resurrected! Even though some of you are feeling like it's been three days.)

Again, we note that post temple, the *matzo* substitutes for the offering of the lamb. The *matzo* is without leaven (sin). It is pierced and striped during the baking process. Jesus, the final sacrifice, was sinless, pierced with a sword and striped by the brutal whipping he received.

> Jesus took bread, gave thanks, broke it, and shared it with them, "This is My body, My body given for you. Do this to remember Me." (Luke 22:19)

The Afikomen is now recovered from its hiding place and returned to the Seder table. Afikomen is a Greek word, from Afikomenos, *meaning, "the coming one." Break the Afikomen into pieces and pass to all.*

ALL. Blessed are you, Lord our God, King of the universe, who brings forth bread from the earth.

All eat the Afikomen matzo.

LEADER.

God promised what he would do for the nation of Israel, and the same promises apply to all who trust in Him.

I will bring you out from under the yoke of the Egyptians. *Now!* "*Come to Me, all who are weary and burdened, and I will give you best. Put My yoke upon your shoulders—it might appear heavy at first, but it is perfectly fitted to your curves. Learn from Me, for I am gentle and humble of heart. When you are yoked to Me, your weary souls will find rest. For My yoke is easy, and My burden is light*" (Matt. 11:28–30).

I will free you from being slaves to the Egyptians. *Now!*

I will free you from being slaves to sin. "*We know this: whatever we used to be with our old sinful ways has been nailed to His cross. So, our entire record of sin has been canceled, and we no longer have to bow down to sin's power*" (Rom. 6:6).

I will redeem you with an outstretched arm and with mighty acts of judgment. *Now!* "*But he was hurt because of us; he suffered so. Our wrongdoing wounded and crushed him. He endured the breaking that made us whole. The injuries he suffered became our healing"* (Isa. 53:5).

I will offer redemption to all through my outstretched arm and through mighty acts. God placed our sin upon Jesus, in our place, redeeming us. Jesus received the judgement that we deserve. This is the ultimate expression of an outstretched arm and a mighty act of judgement.

Raise the third cup of wine and recite:

ALL. Blessed are you, Lord God, King of the universe, Creator of the fruit of the vine.

All drink the third cup of wine.

Elijah, the Herald of the Messiah

LEADER. A place is set at our *Seder* table for the prophet Elijah. In anticipation of his arrival, we have filled his cup with wine. And we will open the door to see if he has arrived.

A young person goes to the front door to see if Elijah has arrived!

The prophet Malachi said that Elijah would arrive to announce the arrival of the Messiah. Jews have been waiting for the Messiah always. They misunderstood what the Messiah's first coming would be about.

John the Baptist was an "Elijah," announcing the *"Lamb sent from God, the sacrifice to erase the sins of the world!" (John 1:29)*. The Jews did not understand and rejected John's announcement. Elijah will come again, as one of the two witnesses during the tribulation period, to announce the soon arrival of the Messiah. The Messiah who will come for the *second time*. This time, however, not as a lamb, but as King of the world!

The Hallel: The Cup of Praise

All fill the fourth cup of wine.

> I will walk among you and be your God,
> and you will be My people. (Lev. 26:12)

READER. This is God's promise, the fourth "I will," promising that he would not only bring the Hebrews out from under the cruel rule of the Egyptians and make them free but that he would do so in a grand and strong fashion. And, finally, God would make the Israelites his own chosen people.

God did deliver the ancient Israelites and (after wandering for forty years because of their disobedience) he did bring them into the land that was promised to Abraham. On Passover, the Jewish people praised God for deliverance that happened thousands of years ago.

How does God take us to be his own people? We, who are Jews, are Jews by birth, though our ethnic bloodline.

We, who are believers, are God's people, by blood, as well as by the shed blood of Jesus. We are adopted into the family of God, by our faith in what his shed blood means.

> *God chose us to be in a relationship with Him even before He laid out plans for this world; He wanted us to live holy lives characterized by love, free from sin, and blameless before Him. (Eph. 1:4)*

Today, we praise God for delivering us from our deserved punishment. We praise him for our anticipated entry into the "Promised

Land" of eternity with him. Let's add a little "Romanized" Greek and shout:

ALL. MARANATHA!

The Hallel: The Praise

LEADER. We return again to the Hallel, Praises to the Lord. We cannot praise him enough for his goodness, faithfulness, mercy, and love for his children, both Jew and Gentile.

The Lord has remembered us. He will bless us. He will bless the house of Israel. He will bless the house of Aaron. He will bless those who revere the Lord, the small as well as the great. May the Lord increase you, more and more, you and your children. You are blessed of the Lord, the maker of heaven and earth. The heavens are the heavens of the Lord, but the earth has he given to the children of men. We will bless the Lord from now and forevermore. Hallelujah!

ALL. Praise the Lord, all you nations. Praise him, all you people, for his mercy prevails over us, as the truth of the Lord endures forever. Hallelujah!

I will praise you, for you have answered and become my deliverance. The stone, which the builders rejected, has become the chief cornerstone. This has proceeded from the Lord; it is marvelous in our eyes.

LEADER. Blessed is he who comes in the name of the Lord. We bless you from the house of the

Lord. O Lord, you are my God, and I will praise you! O my God, I will extol you.

ALL. O our King, for unto you, it is good to give thanks, and pleasant to sing praise unto your name, for you are God from everlasting to everlasting.

All lift their cup of wine and recite:

This is the day which the Lord has appointed.
  We will
rejoice and be glad in it.
Give thanks to the Lord, for he is good, for his
  mercy
endures forever.
Blessed are you, Lord our God, King of the
  universe,
Creator of the fruit of the vine.

All drink the fourth cup of wine.

LEADER. Blessed are you, Lord our God, King of the universe, for the wine and for the fruit of the vine, and for the produce of the field and for that desirable, good and spacious land which you granted our ancestors to inherit, to eat of its fruit, and be satisfied with its goodness.

Have compassion, O Lord our God, upon us, on Israel, your people, upon Jerusalem, your city, on Zion, the residence of your glory, and upon the altar and your temple. Rebuild Jerusalem, your holy city, speedily in our days. Cheer us on this day of the feast of unleavened bread, for you, O

Lord our God, are good and generous to all, and therefore, do we give thanks to you for the land and for the fruit of the vine.

ALL: Blessed are you, O Lord, for the land and for the fruit of the vine.

Together, they all sang a hymn of praise and thanksgiving, and then they took a late evening walk to the Mount of Olives. (Matt. 26:30)

(*Sing the Doxology*)

Praise God, from who all blessings flow.
Praise him, all creatures here below.
Praise him above, ye heavenly host:
Praise Father, Son, and Holy Ghost. Amen.

LEADER: Our *Seder* is now complete. May we all be blessed by having observed this celebration of deliverance. Not just the deliverance of our ancestors from slavery in Egypt, but also the deliverance from God's judgment as provided by the final Passover lamb, *Yeshua Ha Mashiach*, Jesus the Messiah!

Together we proclaim, *"Next year in Jerusalem!"*

Shavuot/Pentecost
Psalm 67

ALL. May God pour his grace and blessing into us and turn his face to shine his light on us.

LEADER. So all those on earth will learn to follow your way and see your saving power come to redeem all nations.

ALL. May all people live to praise you, our true God; may all come to praise you.

LEADER. May all nations celebrate together singing joy-filled songs of praise to you because you judge the people fairly and give guidance to all the nations of the earth.

ALL. May the people praise you with their whole hearts, O God; may every man, woman, and child on the earth praise you.

LEADER. The land has supplied a bountiful harvest, and the true God, our God, has poured out his blessings to us all.

ALL. God is the source of our blessings; may every corner of the earth respect and revere him.

LEADER.

I haven't kept this sacred tithe for myself in my own house. I've given it to the Levites, the foreigners, the orphans, and the widows, just as You commanded me. I haven't broken or forgotten any of Your commands. I haven't eaten any of it while in mourning. I didn't bring any of it here while I was ritually impure, and I haven't offered any of to the dead. I've listened to the voice of the Eternal, my God. I've done everything You commanded me to do. Look down from heaven, from the holy place where You live, and bless Your people Israel and this land flowing with milk and honey, this ground You've given us just as You promised our ancestors. (Deuteronomy 26:13–15)

* Ashkenazi Jews often recite the *Akdamut*—a poem written in Aramaic by Rabbi Meir be Issac Nehorai of Worms, Germany. The poem of praise was written in the form of an acrostic: "Were all the skies parchment and all the reeds pens, all the seas inks and everyone a scribe, God's grandeur still could not be near spilled out."

Sing together "The Love of God."
Verse 3, original Hebrew lyrics by Meir Ben Isaac Nehorai
Words and music by Frederick Martin Lehman

Ten Commandments (Exodus 20:1–17)

(All or alternate around the table.)

1. You are not to serve any other gods before Me.
2. You are not to make any idol or image of other gods. In fact, you are not to make an image of anything in the heavens above, on the earth below, or in the waters beneath. You are not to bow down and serve any image, for I, the Eternal your God, am a jealous God.
3. You are not to use my name for your own idle purposes, for the Eternal will punish anyone who treats His name as anything less than sacred.
4. You and your family are to remember the Sabbath Day; set it apart, and keep it holy.
5. You are to honor your father and mother. If you do, you and your children will live long and well in the land the Eternal has promised to give you.

6. You are not to murder.
7. You are not to commit adultery.
8. You are not to take what is not yours.
9. You are not to give false testimony against your neighbor.
10. You are not to covet what your neighbor has or set your heart on getting his house, wife, servants, animals, or anything else that belongs to your neighbor.

Giving of the Holy Spirit

LEADER. (After the resurrection of Jesus, he appeared to the disciples.)

"May each of you be at peace." As he was speaking, He revealed the wounds in His hands and side. The disciples began to celebrate as it sank in that they were really seeing the Lord. Jesus said, "I give you the gift of peace. In the same way the Father sent Me, I am now sending you." Now He drew close enough to each of them that they could feel His breath. He breathed on them and said, "Welcome the Holy Spirit of the living God." (John 20:20–22)

READER. (Acts 2) The disciples were gathered for the feast of Shavuot. There were people from all over the world who had come to Jerusalem to celebrate this pilgrimage feast. Acts 2 tells the story about the disciples praying and as they prayed, a mighty, rushing wind blew through, and tongues of fire appeared on their heads. They began speaking in other languages, and all the people who heard them understood in their own language! And thus, the church was born! It is important to note that there were Gentiles as well as Jews who heard this.

The inclusion of the Gentiles completed the symbolism of the wave offering, where the High Priest offered two loaves of fine wheat flour baked with leaven. Centuries before, the two loaves of the wave offering symbolized the Body of Messiah made up of both Jewish and Gentile believers. Though the loaves were made of fine wheat flour, they contained leaven, the symbol for sin. That speaks of the fact that the Church, though refined by the blood of the Lamb, still retains the human sin nature until that day when She will be presented as the Bride of Christ, without spot or wrinkle.

Blessing for the meal.

BIBLIOGRAPHY

Bradshaw, Paul F. and Maxwell E. Johnson. *The Origins of Feasts, Fasts and Seasons in Early Christianity*. Collegeville, MN: SPCK, 2011.

Brickner, David. *Christ in the Feast of Tabernacles*. Chicago: Moody, 2006.

Connell, Martin. *Eternity Today: On the Liturgical Year*. vol 1. New York, NY: Continuum, 2006.

Dyrness, William A. *A Primer on Christian Worship*. Grand Rapids, MI and Cambridge, UK: William B. Eerdmans Publishing, 2009.

Hill, Andrew E. *Enter His Courts with Praise: Old Testament Worship for the New Testament Church*. Grand Rapids: Baker Books, 1993.

Kornbluth, Doron. *The Jewish Holiday Handbook*. Mosaica Press, 2014.

Rosen, C. & M. *Christ in the Passover*. Chicago: Moody, 1987.

Shephard, Coulson. *Jewish Holy Days: Their Prophetic and Christian Significance*. Neptune: Loizeaux Bros., 1981.

Sopher, Phil. "Where the 5-Day Workweek Came From." Aug. 21, 2014. (www.theatlantic.com/business/archive/2014/08/where-the-five-day-workweek-came-from/378870/ accessed 6/25/2019).

Stookey, Laurence Hull. *Calendar: Christ's Time for the Church*. Nashville, TN: Abingdon Press, 1996.

The Worship Sourcebook, Grand Rapids. The Calvin Institute of Christian Worship. Faith Alive Christian Resources. Baker Books.

Webber, Robert. *Ancient-Future Time: Forming Spirituality through the Christian Year.* Grand Rapids, MI: Baker Books, 2004. *Ancient-Future Worship.* Grand Rapids: Baker Books, 2008. *Rediscovering the Christian Feasts: A Study in the Services of the Christian Year.* Peabody, MA: Hendrickson, 1998.

Webber, Robert, ed. *The Complete Library of Christian Worship.* Volume I, *The Biblical Foundations of Worship.* Nashville: Star Song Publishing Group, 1993.

Additional Sources Used

Bloch, Abraham P. *The Biblical and Historical Background of the Jewish Customs and Ceremonies.* New York: KTAV Publishing House Inc., 1980.

Rubin, Barry and Steffi Rubin. *The Messianic Passover Haggadah.* Baltimore, MD: The Lederer Foundation 1989.

Stewart-Sykes, Alistair and Judith H. Newman. *Early Jewish Liturgy: A Sourcebook for Use by Students of Early Christian Liturgy.* Ridley Hall Rd. Cambridge: Grove Books Limited, 2001.

Wilkinson, Bruce. *The Three Chairs: Experiencing Spiritual Breakthroughs.* Atlanta, Georgia: Walk Through the Bible Ministries, 2000.

Websites

www.Chabad.org

www.Jamiegeller.com

www.JewsforJesus.org

www.jewlish.com

https://jewishweek.timesofisrael.com/counting-sheep-on-rosh-hashanah/.

https://www.myjewishlearning.com/article/celebrating-sukkot-without-a-sukkah/.

Logos Bible Software—The Lexham Bible Dictionary—Feasts and Festivals of Israel.

www.merriam-webster.com/dictionary/holy%20day
www.toriavey.com
www.whychristmas.com/customs/jessetrees.shtml

Dawn S. Gilmore has a Jewish heritage that comes from her maternal grandfather who, by the grace of God, escaped from the tragedy in Europe and came to America as a young teen. He became a believer in Yeshua, the Messiah, in his late twenties and became an ordained minister. It is from her heritage that Dawn S. Gilmore has developed a particular interest in the biblical feasts and the meaning behind the symbolism.

Dr. Gilmore has been a music educator in Christian schools, worship leader in several denominations, and mentor for over thirty years. She is also a wife, mother, and grandmother who loves to host parties and special events! She received her doctorate of worship studies from the Robert E. Webber Institute of Worship Studies in 2014.

Dr. Gilmore and her retired pastor husband currently live in southern California with their puppy, Asher Lev (Hebrew for *happy heart*), just down the street and around the corner from her Jewish aunt (who is exactly one year older than she) and uncle. They continue to "play house" together just like they did when they were children!

CPSIA information can be obtained
at www.ICGtesting.com
Printed in the USA
LVHW071941260122
709481LV00020B/584

9 781638 854104